PRAISE FOR JACKSON DEAN CHASE

— USA TODAY BESTSELLING AUTHOR —

"[Jackson Dean Chase is] a fresh and powerful new voice."
— Terry Trueman, Printz Honor author of *Stuck in Neutral*

"[Chase] grabs readers from page one."
— Nate Philbrick, author of *The Little One*

"[Jackson Dean Chase] succeeds in taking fiction to a whole new level."
— TheBaynet.com

"[Jackson's fiction is] diligently crafted…"
— The Huffington Post

"Irresistible… [Jackson knows how to write] a heart-pounding story full of suspense, romance, and action!"
— Buzzfeed

MORE BOOKS BY JACKSON DEAN CHASE

WRITING MONSTERS AND MANIACS

A MASTERCLASS IN GENRE FICTION FOR FANTASY, HORROR, AND SCIENCE FICTION

JACKSON DEAN CHASE

WWW.JACKSONDEANCHASE.COM

First printing, June 2018

ISBN-13: 978-1721887811 / ISBN-10: 1721887814

Published by Jackson Dean Chase, Inc.

WRITING MONSTERS AND MANIACS

PUBLISHER'S NOTE

For the monster in me,
and the monster in you.

AUTHOR'S NOTE

As an awkward, unhappy child, I was obsessed with monsters. I identified with them. I wanted to be one, not because I wanted to hurt people, but because I wanted to be powerful enough so people couldn't hurt *me*.

As someone who has experienced what it's like to be an outsider as well as an author and consumer of fantasy, horror, and science fiction, I feel especially qualified to write this book. I've read, watched, and listened to thousands of these stories in all media and written a few of my own...

If you've read my other writing guides, you know what to expect: no fluff, no filler. Just thoughtful, quality content delivered with humor, honesty, and enthusiasm.

— Jackson Dean Chase

P.S.: *The Ultimate Author's Guide to Monsters & Maniacs* was originally published as *How to Write Realistic Monsters, Aliens, and Fantasy Creatures.* For this "ultimate" edition, I've revised and expanded every chapter. There are new monsters and a lot more maniacs! Combined, there's over 30 pages of *exciting new content* for you to enjoy.

WRITING MONSTERS AND MANIACS

INTRODUCTION

HUMANIZING HORROR

MONSTERS. ALIENS. FANTASY CREATURES.

The stuff of nightmares. Science fiction, sword and sorcery, and horror are full of them. Even romance has its share. So why are we so fascinated? Is it because we are compelled to understand our enemies in order to better avoid, tame, or destroy them? Of course. The strange, the exotic, the frightening… these are powerful motivators to provoke curiosity and emotion. But there is another reason we are compelled to study them, a reason few of us dare to admit.

We study them to see our dark side safely reflected in the Other. A funhouse mirror image of what happens when we give in to the darkest impulses of our animal nature. What are monsters if not us? Damned, dead, doomed. Immortal. Invincible. And *free*—at least of society's rules and expectations. That's a powerful attraction, and why we see monsters being humanized in the media.

We are no longer satisfied by simple "evil." We want our monsters complicated, conflicted. *Like us.*

— JACKSON DEAN CHASE
Get a free book at
www.JacksonDeanChase.com

HOW TO USE THIS BOOK

MODIFYING MONSTERS OR MAKING YOUR OWN

IN GENERAL

USE THIS BOOK as a springboard to ensure your monsters are as skillfully written as your human characters. Give them distinct personalities, quirks, and interests apart from just being "evil." For example, when they're not busy murdering people, what do your monsters do to relax? Norman Bates enjoys taxidermy. Buffalo Bill is really into skin lotion and dancing naked to '80s music. Everybody needs a hobby.

I include a list of sample monsters (mostly from movies and TV) so you can see how other writers have handled them. Why didn't I list more books? Because they're not as easy to consume or google reference pictures from. There's less of a chance you'll be familiar with them, and they're harder to fast forward through. Nobody has a problem sitting down to watch a movie or TV show, but the minute you ask them to read a book, resistance goes up. That's why movies and TV are the gold standard for writing references.

I also include a list of plot ideas for most monsters. Feel free to use them "as is," combine them, or change them. To make it easy, I kept the ideas as generic as possible so you can ask yourself, "What if…"

CREATING YOUR OWN MONSTERS

If you are creating a monster from scratch or building off an existing monster type, go to the Appendix and fill in the Monster Builder questionnaire, then consult the Magic Spells, Psychic Talents, and Supernatural Powers sections as needed.

TWEAKING STANDARD MONSTERS

If you just want to give your standard monster a twist, consult the Magic Spells, Psychic Talents, and Supernatural Powers sections in the Appendix, pick what you want, subtract what you don't, and you're good to go!

CREATING MIX-AND-MATCH MONSTERS

Rather than start from scratch, consider mixing and matching different monster types. For example, in the 1977 fantasy adventure film, *Sinbad and the Eye of the Tiger*, instead of just having a standard minotaur, they created a magical robot version called the "Minoton" (minotaur + automaton, get it?). *A Nightmare on Elm Street* (1984) took the concept of a maniac and fused it with a vengeful ghost, making box office magic in the process. This book gives you the tools to do that.

CREATING HALF-BREED MONSTERS

To create a half-breed monster, such as a mix between human and monster, or two different monsters, simply give it some of the powers of each, and maybe an unexpected new one. Similarly, give it only some of the weaknesses of the parents, and maybe a new one. You can also make some of the powers and weaknesses better or worse than is commonly found in its parents.

A popular example of a half-breed is the *dhampir*, the result of either a vampire impregnating a living female, or infecting a pregnant female with vampirism. The resulting child is not undead and can walk in the sunlight, but has some vampire-like qualities. *Blade* (1998) and its sequels provide a good example of this.

ORGANIZED, INTELLIGENT MONSTERS

For Alien and Fantasy Races, as well as Subhumans and any intelligent monster that has its own distinct organized society and culture, I recommend going to the Appendix and answering the Monster Builder questionnaire. This will help you "fill in the blanks" for all those pesky details like what the monsters use for money, what their taboos are, what their language sounds like, etc.

WIZARDS, SORCERERS, WITCHES, AND PRIESTS

I use the terms "wizard" and "sorcerer" interchangeably throughout this book. The term "witch" is used solely to refer to the classic evil witch of horror movies, folklore, and fairy tales, and is not meant to disparage practitioners of Wicca or other Pagan or Neo-Pagan belief systems. The term "priest" is used to refer to a person who performs rituals and services for a religion—in the context of this book, that typically means cults dedicated to alien or malevolent gods or entities.

We can break down the differences between wizards, witches, and priests still further: Wizards learn spells that tap into vast unseen supernatural forces. They are the masters of their own magic.

A priest acts as an intermediary to channel the powers of his gods or entities through religious rituals. The priest knows no spells and has no supernatural power himself, only what his god or spirits grant him.

Witches walk the line between wizard and priest; they have magically bound themselves to a god or entity (perhaps by selling their soul) in exchange for being taught some spells, being granted a demonic familiar, and given supernatural powers which can be taken away if their master becomes displeased (for a good example of this, watch *Salem*, TV, 2014-2017).

GUIDE TO DIFFERENT REALITIES

INTO THE ASTRAL PLANE AND BEYOND

THERE ARE QUITE A FEW TERMS for other realities in this book, particularly in Chapter 3: Energy Beings. Let this guide serve as a quick and easy reference for you .

ALTERNATE REALITY

Also known as an alternative reality or alternate history Earth. An alternate Earth existing in a parallel universe that is in many ways similar to our present, but one in which certain key historical events were altered or never happened. For example, a world where the Axis won World War II. *SS-GB* by Len Deighton and *The Man in the High Tower* by Philip K. Dick are examples of this. See Parallel Universe.

ASTRAL PLANE

Near limitless energy ocean that exists outside the earth and beyond the ethereal plane. Where souls come from and go to. Populated by energy beings (aliens, angels, astral predators, demons, ghosts, etc.). Visited by astral projecting humans.

ETHEREAL PLANE

The Ghost Dimension. Surrounds Earth. Where new souls enter and old souls leave. Populated by energy beings (aliens, ghosts, demons) and visited by astral projecting humans. The ethereal plane feeds off energy beings making it dangerous for them to remain there (including astral projecting humans).

PARALLEL UNIVERSE

Also referred to as a parallel dimension or alternate reality. Similar to an alternate reality, but with no requirement that it be anything like Earth or have anything to do with Earth history or humanity. May be home to aliens, humans, or humanoids.

PHYSICAL PLANE

Includes Earth. Also referred to as reality, physical reality, or physical matter reality. Populated by humans and possibly aliens.

POCKET DIMENSION

An astral kingdom created and ruled by a powerful energy being. It shapes itself according to its ruler's wishes. The kingdom vanishes when the ruler dies or ceases to maintain it. Can be tiny or quite large and populated by thousands or even millions of energy beings (often ghosts who chose to stay here willingly or were tricked into it). There may even be multiple kingdoms sharing the same name to confuse and mislead lost souls, just as there are two towns in the United States calling themselves Kansas City, but only one of them is in Kansas.

THE VOID

A realm of pure darkness where ancient demons are locked away from the rest of the universe. Normally inaccessible.

ALIEN RACES

INTELLIGENT ALIEN RACES with advanced technology present a special problem for authors. Unlike supernatural beings, you can't dismiss what they do as "magic." To be realistic, their technology must be based on science or scientific principles. They also need their own culture, language, and beliefs.

The easiest way to do this is to riff on a human culture. *Star Trek* did it by making the Romulans based on the Roman Empire. You could also base an alien culture around a belief, like the Vulcan belief in promoting logic over emotion, or a rejection of that belief (again using Romulans as an example). You could also take a human warrior code, like Japanese bushido, and use that as the basis for your aliens, like *Star Trek* did with the Klingons.

Another idea is to take a type of animal (such as a tiger), turn it into a humanoid, and begin fleshing out what the world would be like if that was the dominant species instead of man. For an example of this, check out Larry Niven's Kzinti tiger-man species in his novel, *Ringworld*, and short story collection, *The Man-Kzin Wars*.

Physiological details are important. Just as humans snort, sigh, frown, grin, laugh, and cry, so too must your aliens. But how? Come up with different ways they express their emotions. How do they blush? How do they blink? How do they move? How do they express anger, fear, shame, love? What does their language sound like, or are they purely telepathic? Maybe they use pheromones or some other method to communicate. How do they have sex, or do they reproduce another way? Alien habits and gestures must be different, like the Vulcan "live long and prosper" salute.

By consistently reinforcing these differences throughout your story, you will build believability into your alien species. But you also need to build reader empathy, and the more alien you make them, the harder that is to do. So don't just think of ways your alien is different, but think of ways they are like humans.

WRITING RELATABLE ALIENS

What do your aliens have in common with humanity? What do we share with them that does not need a translator to interpret? What can we bond over? These are important questions you need to ask yourself. If your answer is "nothing," then readers may have a hard time understanding and appreciating your aliens. Yes, aliens should be different, but they should also be the same in some ways. This applies to both heroes and villains, from *Star Trek*'s Mr. Spock to the charming and despicable Leader Desslok of *Star Blazers*.

Perhaps the two best examples of turning a stock alien into a three-dimensional character that we can relate to and root for are the 1985 sci-fi film, *Enemy Mine*, and "The Return of Starbuck" episode of *Galactica 1980*. In both examples, a human hero gets in a dogfight with a skilled alien pilot. The fight ends in a draw as both pilots shoot each other down. Although initially hostile, relations warm once they realize they are stranded and must cooperate to survive.

The primary difference between the two scenarios is that in the *Galactica 1980* episode, the enemy pilot is a Cylon robot the hero salvages from the crashed ship. He decides to repair it out of boredom, knowing it's a bad idea and the Cylon will try to kill him. But what else can he do? He needs to talk to somebody, and even an emotionless, human- hating "toaster" is better than nothing.

One more way to create a relatable alien is to make him "one of us," like how Superman was raised by humans and assimilated into our culture. This is easier when the aliens appear and act human or human-like, such as the crew in *Farscape* (TV, 1999-2003), or when they embody familiar aspects of our culture, such as the ancient Egyptian-inspired aliens from *Stargate* (1994).

Once you've created the basic template for your alien race, you need to decide how to differentiate one alien from another. Just as each human may share certain cultural beliefs and genetic traits, attitudes and opinions can vary wildly, diverging in a million ways. That's where the gold is!

WRITING ALIEN OR FANTASY LANGUAGES

There are two tricks you can employ when writing alien or fantasy languages. The first is to use just a few of these words sparingly and render them in italics. You then have to find an elegant way to explain what those words mean to your readers. Try to keep the new words short and easy to pronounce, like *"Glish-ka!"* or *"No'rathma, ven."*

The second trick is simply to write the language in English, but surround the dialogue with either < > or << >> and, when first used, an explanation that the character is speaking another language. For example: <<Off-world scum,>> the alien cursed in its native tongue. << You think you own this world!>>

If your alien doesn't speak, or only communicates through growls or pheromones, you will need to include a character who can interpret for them, as Han Solo does for Chewbacca in *Star Wars* (1977). When their interpreter is absent, that can create fun tension when the alien tries to communicate with the crew who can't understand it.

For these aliens, you will need to create some kind of physical and/or vocal shorthand that illustrates the intent (or emotion) behind their communication, such as:

- The Wookie grunted, shrugging its massive shoulders.
- The fish-man flared his gills is disdain.

SAMPLE ALIENS

- *The Day the Earth Stood Still* (1951)
- *Invaders from Mars* (1953 and 1986 remake)
- *War of the Worlds* (1953 and 2005 remake)
- *Earth vs. the Flying Saucers* (1956)
- *Invasion of the Body Snatchers* (1956 and 1978 remake)
- *Invasion of the Saucer Men* (1957)
- *The Blob* (1958 and 1988 remake)
- *I Married a Monster from Outer Space* (1958)
- *It! The Terror from Beyond Space* (1958)
- *Star Trek* (TV, 1966-69)
- *The Invaders* (TV, 1967-68)
- *The Green Slime* (1968)
- *The Alien Factor* (1978)
- *Close Encounters of the Third Kind* (1977)
- *Message from Space* (1978)
- *Superman* (1978)
- *Alien* (1979)
- *Star Blazers* (TV, 1979-82)
- *Battle Beyond the Stars* (1980)
- *Superman 2* (1980)
- *The Deadly Spawn* (1983)
- *V* (TV miniseries, 1983, TV series 1984-85)
- *The Last Starfighter* (1984)
- *Voltron, Defender of the Universe* (TV, 1984-85)
- *Alien Predator* (1985, aka *Alien Predators*)
- *Enemy Mine* (1985)
- *Aliens* (1986)
- *Critters* (1986)
- *The Hidden* (1987)
- *Predator* (1987)
- *Star Trek: The Next Generation* (TV, 1987-94)
- *Killer Klowns from Outer Space* (1988)

- *War of the Worlds* (TV, 1988-90)
- *Alien Nation* (1988 and TV series, 1989-90)
- *Communion* (1989)
- *I Come in Peace* (1990)
- *Fire in the Sky* (1993)
- *Star Trek: Deep Space Nine* (TV, 1993-99)
- *Stargate* (1994)
- *Species* (1995)
- *Contact* (1997)
- *Starship Troopers* (1997)
- *Farscape* (TV, 1999-2003)
- *District 9* (2009)
- *The Fourth Kind* (2009)
- *Monsters* (2010)
- *Skyline* (2010)
- *Falling Skies* (TV, 2011-15)
- *Guardians of the Galaxy* (2014)
- *Infini* (2015)
- *Arrival* (2016)
- *The 5th Wave* (2016)
- *Life* (2017)
- *Annihilation* (2018)

ALIEN PLOT IDEAS

1. An alien EMP takes out all the electricity on Earth.
2. A man abducted by aliens tries to prove he's not insane.
3. Aliens take over the minds of everyone in a small town.
4. Aliens hunt humans for sport in a remote setting.
5. Captured alien monsters (zoological specimens) escape from a crashed starship and terrorize a community.
6. An alien bounty hunter teams up with a human cop.
7. An alien energy being uses its psychic powers to take over a human in order to experience what having a body is like.

2

ANIMALS

CRYPTIDS, TOTEM ANIMALS, WILD AND DOMESTIC ANIMALS

IF YOU ARE LOOKING for mythological beasts, refer to Chapter 4. If you are looking for mutant or radioactive animals, refer to Chapter 7.

CRYPTIDS

Cryptids are animals whose existence is disputed and remains unproven. They are the subject of hoaxes for fame and financial gain. Are these creatures real? Are they evolutionary holdovers from prehistoric times, or are they aliens, mutants, or something else?

BIGFOOT, SKUNK APE, AND YETI

Bigfoot is a hairy, ape-like humanoid that roams the mountains and forests of the Pacific Northwest. It is known to Native Americans by its Salish name, Sasquatch ("wild man"), and has a history going back hundreds of years. A similar monster called the Skunk Ape has been reported in the Arkansas, Florida, and North Carolina swamps. It is known for its horrible smell. The Yeti is a white-furred, ape-like humanoid that lives in the mountains of Nepal.

All of these cryptids are taller than a man and more powerfully built. They walk on two legs, not four, and their arms are long, their hands coming to their knees when they walk. These cryptids avoid humans, but are deadly if threatened. They live in remote, often inaccessible wilderness, only ranging into human areas in search of food or to flee some natural disaster.

On a larger scale, both *King Kong* (1933) and *Mighty Joe Young* (1949) could be considered cousins to Bigfoot and the Yeti.

CHUPACABRA

The chupacabra (literally "goatsucker" in Spanish) is a hairless, dog-like creature with spines running down its back. It drinks blood and was first reported in Puerto Rico in 1995. Eight sheep were found dead, drained of blood, with three puncture wounds in each body. Chupacabra sightings have since been reported all over the world.

JERSEY DEVIL

The Jersey Devil is a flying dragon-like creature with red eyes, the head of a goat, clawed hands, a forked tail, cloven hooves, and leathery wings. It is supposedly immortal and lives in the Pine Barrens of New Jersey. It was first reported in 1735, and said to be the 13th child of Deborah Leeds, in the community of Leeds Point. The devil killed the midwife and flew up the chimney, then terrorized the community.

In 1740, the Jersey Devil was exorcised by a priest. No further sightings occurred until 1820. There were several more sightings throughout the 1800s, but over two hundred occurred in 1909, sending the entire state into a "devil panic."

LOCH NESS MONSTER

Scotland is allegedly home to a long-necked sea dragon or plesiosaur nicknamed, "Nessie." The first report of its existence was in the 6th century, but a blurry photograph in 1933 made the monster famous. The photo was a hoax, but belief in the creature continues.

SAMPLE CRYPTIDS

- *King Kong* (1933 and 1976 and 2005 remakes)
- *Mighty Joe Young* (1949 and 1998 remake)
- *The Abominable Snowman (1957)*
- *The Legend of Boggy Creek* (1972)
- *The Mysterious Monsters* (Documentary, 1976)
- *The Crater Lake Monster* (1977)
- *Night of the Demon* (1980)
- *The Loch Ness Horror* (1981)
- *Harry and the Hendersons* (1987)
- *Chupacabra Terror* (2005)
- *The Barrens* (2012)
- *Willow Creek* (2013)
- *Dark Was the Night* (2014)
- *Exists* (2014)

CRYPTID PLOT IDEAS

1. Campers violate the territory of one or more cryptids.
2. A cryptid seeks a human to mate with.
3. Cryptids attack when civilization encroaches on them.
4. A cryptid causes mysterious livestock mutilations.
5. Professional "monster hunters" hunt cryptids.
6. Mad scientists turn humans into cryptids.
7. The military creates cryptid super-soldiers.
8. Cryptids are actually were-creatures, turning from humans into monsters during mating season.
9. Locals fake a cryptid sighting to increase tourism.
10. A TV crew arrives to document cryptid sightings.
11. Cryptozoologists want to verify the local cryptids.
12. Locals ward off cryptids by sacrificing tourists to them.
13. Diseased cryptids infect a rural community.

TOTEM ANIMALS

To inject an element of myth, magic, and the supernatural into an animal story, you can have totem animals (also known as "spirit animals") appear. These are impossibly perfect paragons of their species, larger than normal, and often white or another rare or unheard-of color.

White is the color of purity and otherworldliness (at least to white people). Other races may perceive the animal to be black or another color that represents these same qualities to them.

The white stag of England is one of the best known European totem animals, as is the unicorn (some consider them the same creature). Totem animals may have personal names or be known by their species name, such as "Brother Wolf."

Totem animals are part of animism (also called shamanism or totemism), which are the religious beliefs of indigenous peoples. Animism believes everything has a spirit, from rocks to trees to animals to weather, as well as land and sea, the sky, and Earth itself.

Totem animals are considered divine, the equivalent of major spirits or minor gods. They may exist in the physical world temporarily or permanently, and may have a physical body or only an energy body, or perhaps they have both due to the totem spirit possessing a real animal. In any case, there is rarely more than one in existence in our reality at a time. A totem animal has complete telepathic command and control of natural animals of its species.

Totem animals may be summoned through shamanic ritual or appear as a spirit guide or warning when humanity is about to transgress a spiritual boundary or taboo.

SAMPLE TOTEM ANIMALS

- *The White Buffalo* (1977)
- *The Prophecy* (1978)
- *Nightwing* (1979)

- *Wolfen* (1981)
- *The Last Unicorn* (1982)
- *Q* (1982, aka *Q—the Winged Serpent*)
- *Spasms* (1983)
- *Legend* (1985)
- *Lair of the White Worm* (1988)
- *Balto II: Wolf Quest* (2002)
- *Brother Bear* (2003)
- *Cry of the Winged Serpent* (2007)

TOTEM ANIMAL PLOT IDEAS

1. A ruthless big game hunter stalks a totem animal.
2. A shaman summons totem animals to stop a corporation from stealing or polluting tribal land.
3. A shaman takes on the shape of a totem animal for revenge.
4. A totem animal takes on physical form to punish those who killed its kind or harmed its tribe.
5. A totem animal attacks those who disturb sacred ground.

WILD AND DOMESTIC ANIMALS

Jaws. Cujo. The Rats. Killer critters made popular by books and films. You may be wondering how you can possibly make a "regular" predatory beast exciting compared to its mythological or mutant brethren. Like any good villain, you need to get inside its head and see through its eyes. That's what Peter Benchley did in *Jaws*, what Stephen King did in *Cujo*, and what James Herbert did in *The Rats*. Animal POV isn't rocket science, but it does take getting used to.

So how does the animal view the world? Through smell, more than anything. That's how it knows what is safe, what is dangerous, and what is prey. An animal who smells fear knows it has the upper hand and is likely to attack or assert its dominance.

Keep its emotions basic, primal. Focus on smells and sounds more than what it sees. Remember, an animal can't tell the difference between a stick and rifle until someone pulls the trigger. It doesn't worry about anything but food, shelter, sex, and fun (or companionship, if it's a pack animal, or one that mates for life).

As for what it sees, it will have a limited understanding of any man-made items or environments; it is likely to express curiosity, confusion, fear, anger, or annoyance with them until it is satisfied how "safe" the man-made thing or area is.

On the other hand, an animal has an excellent understanding of its natural habitat. It will feel comfortable there, knowing where to hide, where to hunt, and where to sleep, unless that environment has been disturbed, typically by the actions of men. The animal may flee, retreat, or decide to confront those disturbing its environment.

Animals fleeing their home due to the encroachment of men or in response to a natural disaster will make an effective plot, as can animals taking over the ruins after a nuclear war.

Dangerous animals could escape from a circus or shelter and rampage through a neighborhood, trapping people in their houses as a man-eating tiger does in the 2010 thriller, *Burning Bright*. Even a normally friendly domestic animal can be trained to be vicious (or situationally vicious), like in *White Dog* (1982).

Other ways to make animals more frightening is to give them a disease such as rabies, as Stephen King did in his novel, *Cujo*, or bubonic plague as Martin Cruz Smith gave the bats in his novel, *Nightwing*. If you want to get really out there, you could feed an entire zoo mind-bending drugs that make the animals go berserk, as in the 1984 horror film, *The Wild Beasts*.

Animals can be be used as a method of revenge by human maniacs, such as in *Willard* (1971) and its sequel, *Ben* (1972), *Stanley* (1972), *Pigs* (1973), *Eaten Alive* (1976), *Jennifer* (1978), and *Shark Night 3D* (2011).

You could opt to have animals controlled by magical, psychic, or scientific means. In the 1978 horror film, *Jennifer*, a teenage girl from a snake-handling cult discovers she can telepathically control snakes. Naturally, she uses them to get revenge on those who did her wrong.

Finally, there's the tried and true method of making animals bigger than usual, like the giant crocodile in *Lake Placid* (1999), prehistoric, like the shark in *The Meg* (2018), or simply meaner, like the shark in *Jaws* (1975). Mutating them by radiation is popular, and so are shapeshifters. See the mutants and shapeshifters chapters.

SAMPLE WILD AND DOMESTIC ANIMALS

- *The Birds* (1963)
- *The Deadly Bees* (1966)
- *Eye of the Cat* (1969)
- *Willard* (1971 and 2003 remake)
- *Ben* (1972)
- *Frogs* (1972)
- *Night of a Thousand Cats* (1972)
- *Stanley* (1972)
- *Pigs* (1973)
- *Chosen Survivors* (1974)
- *Jaws* (1975)
- *Eaten Alive* (1976)
- *Grizzly* (1976)
- *Mako: The Jaws of Death* (1976)
- *Rattlers* (1976)
- *The Savage Bees* (TV, 1976)
- *Squirm* (1976)
- *Ants* (1977)
- *Day of the Animals* (1977)
- *Kingdom of the Spiders* (1977)
- *Orca* (1977)
- *Tentacles* (1977)
- *Jaws 2* (1978)
- *Jennifer* (1978)
- *The Pack* (1978)
- *The Swarm* (1978)
- *Tarantulas: The Deadly Cargo* (TV, 1978)

- *Terror Out of the Sky* (TV, 1978)
- *Roar* (1981)
- *Venom* (1981)
- *Deadly Eyes* (1982)
- *White Dog* (1982)
- *Cujo* (1983)
- *Jaws 3D* (1983)
- *Razorback* (1984)
- *The Wild Beasts* (1984)
- *Phenomena* (1985, aka *Creepers*)
- *Dark Age* (1987)
- *Monkey Shines* (1988)
- *Strays* (1991)
- *Outbreak* (1995)
- *The Ghost and the Darkness* (1996)
- *Anaconda* (1997)
- *Lake Placid* (1999)
- *Open Water* (2003)
- *Snakes on a Plane* (2006)
- *Rogue* (2007)
- *Burning Bright* (2010)
- *Shark Night 3D* (2011)
- *The Reef* (2010)
- *Backcountry* (2014)
- *The Shallows* (2016)
- *47 Meters Down* (2017)
- *The Meg* (2018)

ANIMAL PLOT IDEAS

1. One or more animals contract a deadly disease.
2. Zoo or circus animals escape and go on a rampage.
3. Packs of wild animals hunt humans after a nuclear war.
4. A telepathic human controls animals for revenge.

3

ENERGY BEINGS

ASTRAL PREDATORS, DEMONS, GHOSTS (INCLUDING POSSESSION)

BEFORE WE BEGIN TALKING about Energy Beings, it's important to understand where they come from, and to do that, we need to create a basic understanding of where and how they exist.

I'm not going to make this a religious debate; that's not the point of this book. You can simplify things to just Heaven, Hell, and Limbo (the Astral or Ethereal planes). You could use the Greek underworld of Tartarus or the Norse heaven of Valhalla. It really doesn't matter what you call these places or what religious lens you filter them through.

The point of including this background information is so you can have easy, ready to go rules and settings. *If you prefer to make up your own afterlife and inter-dimensional travel rules, go ahead.* I am going to provide the basic system I use in my fiction as a frame of reference. Feel free to customize it to your liking, mix-and-match with your own ideas, or throw out whatever you don't like or agree with.

THE ASTRAL AND ETHEREAL PLANES

Energy beings come from the astral plane or the ethereal plane. Gods, angels, demons, astral predators, and even some alien races come from the astral plane. Ghosts, however, come from the ethereal plane, and some types of corporeal undead draw their power from there as well. That's not to say you can't encounter ghosts in the astral plane. Any human soul that escapes the ethereal can choose to wander the astral plane instead, though that can be even more dangerous, since the astral is home to all manner of energy beings eager to take advantage of unwary "lost souls."

The astral plane is outside the Earth, while the ethereal plane surrounds the Earth. It is possible to cross from the astral to the ethereal or vice versa, just as it is possible to travel from either of them to Earth. Energy beings that come to Earth enter the ethereal plane first. Being ethereal, energy beings are naturally invisible on Earth and must expend energy to activate their powers, much less manifest them in a physical sense or to possess the living.

When humans die, our souls go to the ethereal plane. This is supposed to be a brief layover before moving on to the astral plane, then back to our Creator, Source, God, gods, or whatever you want to call where we come from or what made us. Whether that destination is our final one or just a brief vacation before we reincarnate is up to you.

When human souls refuse to move on (for whatever reason), they get stuck in the ethereal plane. I go into detail about this in the Ghosts section, so I want to focus on summing up the astral plane here:

The astral plane is a vast energy ocean, a near-limitless expanse that connects to every dimension and every world. It is home to spirits of all kinds, but may only be visited by humans through astral projection, dreams, or near-death experience.

The barrier between physical reality and the astral plane is difficult to cross for both humans and spirits. It requires tremendous psychic energy and skill to accurately project. That amount of energy is reduced for spirits who have possessed a human through which they can draw the required energy.

Strong human emotions release psychic energy that may be fed upon by spirits to enter and manifest themselves in our world. That is why they are so desirous for human contact.

ASTRAL PREDATORS

Astral predators (sometimes called "astral vampires") are natives to the astral plane. They are energy beings that can take on one or more shapes, usually alien and frightening. Some may appear as humanoid shadows with red eyes, others as hideous shadow hybrids of bats, rats, lions, insects, snakes, worms, eels, octopi, sharks, or wolves. These are nightmare images pulled from their victim's minds, for their true forms are always vague, amorphous gray ooze, a kind of psychic amoeba.

Astral predators possess an animal cunning, relentlessly stalking and terrorizing their prey to feed on the resulting negative energy (anger, fear, etc.). They have no discernible language and understand only brute force. They may be encountered singly or in packs, but they avoid beings who appear stronger than them.

Astral predators feed on other astral lifeforms, but their favorite food are humans using astral projection. Most humans do not realize they are astral projecting and think they are dreaming, which makes them easy prey to astral predators.

As an added bonus, humans can't be drained dry by them in one meal like lesser astral lifeforms. That means humans are a self-replenishing food source—the perfect meal. Once the predator scores a successful attack on a human, it acts like a tracking device, an anchor the predator can use to always find (and feed on) that particular human again.

Predators have no interest in possessing the living because they have no use for a physical host body. They are not intelligent enough to know how to feed on energy through anyone but their host, so the idea of "trapping" themselves in a living body has no value to them.

The only ways to rid yourself of an astral predator are to scare it off with a show of psychic or magical force, or by feeding it positive emotions, which cause it to sicken and flee (or die, if you can hold it in place long enough).

Once the predator determines you are no longer safe or appetizing, it immediately removes its psychic anchor, severing the connection, and flees as far and as fast as it can. Once driven away, predators instinctively know to avoid that individual or group in the future.

Variant astral predators may mutate, acquiring the intelligence and skills of those they feed on. They can then take on new shapes, including the appearances of those they have tasted or consumed.

A mutant who eats enough magicians, psychics, or other skilled (or interesting) humans may develop an unhealthy interest in learning more of our world. It will be completely amoral and insane, seeing humans as not only food, but as playthings to bring it new toys and amusing experiences. The mutant may be fixated on specific aspects of humanity, such as sexuality or suffering, or it may enjoy battles of wits or physical contests, all of which are new to it.

Left unchecked, these mutants could grow powerful enough to begin eating energy beings like angels or demons, acquiring their knowledge and abilities, and eventually becoming god-like abominations. Such mutants typically end up creating and ruling over their own twisted astral kingdoms, tricking and enslaving lost souls or astral travelers into entering their domain, only to never let them leave.

Astral predators cannot be summoned in the usual ways. They have no personal names or sigils to call, no masters to entreat. They are attracted to open gates where the borders between the astral, ethereal, and physical planes merge.

Astral predators in this spillover zone between realities take on more real and defined shapes, losing their shadowy substance and becoming more flesh-like. This is not a good thing! Although now they are subject to physical attacks rather than only psychic or magical ones, their own attacks now affect living bodies—not just feeding on energy, but brutally maiming or killing. Their *intent* is still to feed, but they cannot understand why their prey keeps running out of energy so fast (as in dying).

As soon as the gate closes, the predators are sucked back through to the astral plane. They cannot remain or venture outside the boundaries of the astral spillover.

SAMPLE ASTRAL PREDATORS

- *From Beyond* (1986)
- *The Void* (2016)

ASTRAL PREDATOR PLOT IDEAS

1. Mad scientists or wizards open a gate that lets astral predators into our reality.
2. An untrained psychic accidentally opens a gate to astral predators while dreaming.
3. A mutant astral predator passes itself off as a different monster or god to trick new victims.
4. A man in a coma astral projects himself into the pocket dimension of a mutant astral predator.
5. Your hero moves to a house on a rift between dimensions that allows astral predators in.

DEMONS

"Demon" is a catch-all term for any astral energy being that is neutral or actively hostile toward humanity, regardless of whether the being in question is actually "evil" or not. By presenting themselves as obstacles, we *perceive* them to be evil, and what we do not understand, we fear.

However, for the purpose of this book, we will be dealing with one particular type of energy being in all its variations: the traditional demons most popular in fiction. I won't go into any particular religion (you are free to layer in those details yourself). Instead, I am going to present a working system for classifying and creating demons suitable for any religion or no religion. There are a lot of story worlds out there, and I want this book to be useful to as many writers as possible. Feel free to change or ignore what you want.

WHAT ARE DEMONS?

Demons are soulless, genderless immortal energy beings akin to spiritual parasites or "vampires" that appear as blobs, smears, shadows, haze, or fog. Their colors are their auras, energy fields that surround them and reveal their true nature: dead black, dull gray, sickly brown, dirty yellow, cancerous orange, angry red, nauseous green, violent purple. To avoid giving themselves away, they disguise themselves with illusions drawn from the minds of their enemies. These will either be seductive or nightmarish depending on the demon's purpose.

Demons have never been "alive" in a physical sense; they have no soul. Their thoughts and actions are alien, capricious, often malevolent. They come from dark places, cold places, despising light and warmth. These places have been called Hell, because they are hell to humans. They are also hell to demons, who see possessing humans as an opportunity to take a vacation from their torment.

Even the weakest demon sees itself as superior to the strongest human. They regard us as playthings, chess pieces to be moved about then cast aside when the game no longer interests them. And they don't like losing!

DEMONIC POWERS

All demons share the same standard set of strengths and weaknesses. The more powerful demons (tempters or higher) will have more psychic powers, more supernatural powers, and will know a variety of magic spells.

STANDARD DEMON PSYCHIC TALENTS

- Alter Emotion (one step at a time)
- Alter Perceptions/Senses of Others (Create hallucinations)
- Astral Projection

- Clairaudience (Hear what others are saying far away)
- Clairvoyance (See what others are doing far away)
- Enhanced Senses (Cannot be surprised, etc.)
- ESP (Extra-Sensory Perception)
- Influence Others (Implant Hypnotic Suggestions)
- Locate Energy Beings and Hide from Same
- Postcognition (Ability to see events after they have happened)
- Precognition (Ability to see events before they happen)
- Psychokinesis (aka telekinesis, the ability to move objects with the mind)
- Read Auras
- Telepathy (One-way or two-way)
- Trilocation (Ability to be in three places at the same time: astral, ethereal, and physical planes)

STANDARD DEMON SUPERNATURAL STRENGTHS

- Immortality
- Invisible to Humans
- Levitation
- Summon Demons

STANDARD DEMON SUPERNATURAL WEAKNESSES

- Believes Itself and/or Its Kind Superior to Humans
- Cannot Cross Running Water (except by bridge, boat, etc.)
- Cannot Enter a Private Residence without Being Invited by a Living Owner or Guest
- Cannot Enter Holy Ground
- Cannot Speak Holy Names
- Hurt by Holy Objects
- Hurt by Iron

- Hurt by Sunlight
- Must Feed on Psychic Energy (subtly on Earth, more dramatically in the astral plane)
- Must Keep Its Oath or Promise (if magically bound)
- Must Rest in Its Native Plane to Recharge Its Powers
- Repelled by Holy Objects
- Repelled by Love and/or Positive Emotions
- Repelled by Salt
- Repelled by Water

From weakest to most powerful, here is a list of demons:

FAMILIAR DEMONS (MINOR DEMON)

Below even the rank of minor demons are familiar demons (sometimes called imps); they are assigned by tempter or higher ranking demons to aid and advise witches.

Familiars are unable to possess humans but will possess a small animal, such as a bat, rat, cat, dog, frog, raven, snake, or spider so as to be able to physically interact with the world on their master's behalf, as well as to drink the blood of their witch. They are generally poor combatants and best used as spies.

Familiars also serve as a combination homing beacon and psychic anchor (like a cellphone tower) that make it easier for the master to keep tabs on and communicate with the witch.

When necessary, the master can also channel a fraction of its power through the familiar without personally having to be present. This is another reason covens of witches (each with their own familiar) are so dangerous. Provided they all belong to the same master, the familiars can combine their fractions of power into a single, full strength effect as if the master itself were present.

Goals and Motivations: Serving their master is the first priority of familiars; serving their assigned witch is important, but secondary.

TERROR DEMONS (MINOR DEMON)

These low-ranking brutes use fear and horror to terrorize humans. They are not particularly intelligent, but they are cunning and good at what they do. To inspire fear, they take on the appearance of nightmare fusions of beast and man.

When asked what they want, terror demons issue short, hateful replies, such as "You will die!" and "We will kill you!" They are hoping to feed on the negative psychic energy their tactics are designed to produce. If those fail to get a result, they will try to escalate things through violence (throwing furniture around, pushing people down the stairs, etc.). If that *still* does not achieve their goals, they will call in reinforcements of their own kind or a Tempter demon to switch tactics.

When demons are suspected of haunting a house or possessing a human, it is usually this kind that are responsible. A house or other area haunted by them will be abnormally dark and cold, giving off "bad vibes." Someone possessed by terror demons gains super-strength and becomes violent. Note that like ghosts, there is no limit to the number of minor demons that can possess a human.

Goals and Motivations: Causing harm and spreading fear is all that matters to terror demons.

TEMPTER DEMONS (MAJOR DEMON)

Owing to their higher intelligence, these demons use ambition, greed, and seduction to broker deals for human souls. They appear as regal and diabolical humanoids but can take on more frightening forms when angered. They are harder to trick and harder to exorcise than terror demons. Their intimidating presence bolsters the strength of any lesser demons present.

There are fewer of them, so it is rare to find more than one possessing a single human. Even when they do possess one, it is usually only on a temporary basis, to ensure some task gets done that cannot be entrusted to its terror demon underlings.

When they run into a problem they can't solve, they will call in reinforcements (either more terror demons or other tempters), or they may choose to escalate things by calling in a demon prince. This can be a risky strategy, as the prince may be displeased with having to come handle matters, and that displeasure will be taken out as punishment on all the other demons present. The prince is under no compulsion to appear, however.

Goals and Motivations: Corrupting and seducing humans into evil ways to gain their souls is the primary goal of tempter demons. A human possessed by one becomes charming, amoral, and manipulative. Tempter demons may initially appear less threatening because they have a greater level of patience and self-control than terror demons, but they have no problem resorting to violence if in danger of losing.

SORCERER DEMONS (MAJOR DEMON)

A sorcerer demon stands outside the demonic hierarchy as a (more or less) free agent. It is not a true demon, but rather a human sorcerer who has fused its soul with the same essence of darkness that demons are born from. The sorcerer may have achieved this on its own or by making a pact with a demon god. Rather than return to its source for its reward and/or reincarnation, the sorcerer's soul has elected to remain in the astral plane.

The sorcerer demon will appear as a more fearsome version of how it appeared in life, but may have learned to take on other forms as well. It has access to all the memories it had when alive, plus its psychic abilities and magic spells as well as the standard supernatural abilities of demons. Some liches (see the Undead chapter) become sorcerer demons once their undead bodies are destroyed.

Sorcerer demons go where they want and can return to Earth without being summoned. They may build and rule astral kingdoms by creating "pocket dimensions." Or they may wander the astral plane, exploring other worlds and realities.

Because they retain their human identity (if not their humanity), they may be more inclined to help or at least listen to human astral travelers in need, or to entertain them as their "guests" in exchange for information about what's going on back on Earth. They may also be more favorably disposed toward fellow sorcerers or those of their human bloodline.

Goals and Motivations: Knowledge is the most important thing to sorcerer demons, though they will have other interests as well. Note that while sorcerer demons can *attempt* to summon other demons, without a prior arrangement, no demons are under obligation to appear, let alone obey, the sorcerer demon. Sorcerer demons therefore magically bind lesser demons into service to have "on stand-by," or else they will make quid pro quo alliances.

DEMON PRINCES (MAJOR DEMON)

These are demonic nobility, either naturally occurring (such as a fallen angel) or raised up from the ranks of tempter demons for exceptional service. They have all the powers of tempter and terror demons, plus they have additional powers and know most or all magic spells. Princes appear however they wish, but tend to have a preferred appearance (at least when dealing with humans). They command legions of terror and tempter demons.

Princes rarely possess humans except the rich and powerful (generals, billionaires, and politicians are their favorites). Unlike lower ranking demons, princes can possess multiple humans at the same time.

A prince can summon vast numbers of lesser demons as well as its god though it seldom does so for fear of looking weak and being punished, or worse, demoted. Further, the god is under no obligation to appear.

Goals and Motivations: Princes are a combination of general, high priest, and ambassador for their god. They seek to expand their god's kingdom, as well as their own fortunes. Some scheme to replace their god, and from time to time, some succeed.

DEMON GODS (MAJOR DEMON)

These are self-styled "gods," the most powerful of their kind, each with their own interests, powers, and goals. They can appear however they wish, from beautiful to horrifying to utterly alien. Like princes, they have a preferred form when dealing with humans. Their power is so great that they cannot remain long when possessing a human vessel, splitting it apart. Like princes, gods have the ability to possess multiple humans at the same time.

Each god reigns over its own noble court of princes and underlings. These courts are built according to the demon god's whims and are as complicated and full of intrigue as any human court. They exist in a series of interconnected pocket dimensions (kingdoms) that collectively make up what humans refer to as "Hell." Note that Hell is cold and dark by nature, and anything to the contrary is an illusion or temporary construct made possible by the demon god exerting its will upon the energy of the place.

Variant demon gods include the ultra-powerful alien beings of H.P. Lovecraft's Cthulhu Mythos. These beings do not come from Hell, but from other realities or dimensions. They see humanity as little better than insects but freely make bargains and accept worship if it gains them some advantage or amusement. Variant demon gods can be briefly summoned to Earth in physical form (usually hideous and madness-inducing to behold). They are powerful psychics and sorcerers.

Goals and Motivations: Whether of the variant variety or not, all demon gods are interested in maintaining and expanding their power by any means necessary.

VOID DEMONS (MAJOR DEMON)

These are ancient and powerful demons that existed in the icy void before the creation of the universe. They were displaced by the coming of light, life, and heat. All other demons fear them, and while some work toward their return, others actively oppose that goal, as it would mean a reduction in their own personal power. Void demons have been magically sealed away by the forces of Light. The only time they are encountered is when that seal weakens, allowing a small part of their evil to slip through.

Goals and Motivations: Void demons plot to restore endless darkness to the universe by destroying it.

DEMONIC NAMES, SUMMONING, AND PACTS

Knowledge is power. Every demon has a personal "true" name that allows anyone who knows it to command them. Because of this, demons employ various pseudonyms so they can be summoned but not commanded. These pseudonyms are the names most commonly found in spell books.

Summoning demons without knowing their true name requires you to make a quid pro quo pact to get them to do your bidding. If you have not properly protected yourself by summoning the demon into a magic circle, it is under no obligation to negotiate and can simply leave or try to murder you. Even if you make a pact, demons attempt to fulfill the letter of the agreement, *never* your intent.

Note that a demon can only do what is within the scope of its natural, psychic, and magical abilities—nothing more. So if you ask a demon for a million dollars, it can't create it out of thin air. It's going to steal that money and bring it to you. Unless you've told it to make sure there is *no trace* linking the theft back to you, you can rest assured the demon will find a way to implicate you in the crime. That's why you must be extremely careful and clever making pacts.

Let's take a quick look at four ways a demon might creatively interpret a pact with a human wishing for immortality:

1. The human body cannot live forever, but the human soul can. So the most expedient way for the demon to honor this pact (or some other pact that goes beyond the bargainer's lifespan) is for it to simply kill the pact-maker and show them their soul is immortal. Problem solved, pact fulfilled!

2. The demon could take the human's soul after death (it would be a ghost at this point) and place it into another human body. If that body has a soul in it already, then a contest of wills takes place, with the ghost vying to possess, dominate, and cast out the original soul (perhaps aided by the demon). A comatose body whose body has abandoned it, or the body of someone astral projecting (whose soul is temporarily in the astral plane) would be the ideal host body, since the ghost could just walk right in and take over. The pact-maker now understands how to "live forever" on Earth, so the demon's obligation is done.

3. If magic is prevalent in your story world, the demon could locate and present the pact-maker with a spell to attain lichdom (see Lich in the Undead chapter), or a ritual to turn them into a demon-sorcerer.

4. If undead are present in your story world, the pact-maker could be turned into one of those upon death. The demon may arrange for the pact-maker to be murdered by an undead (and thus infected), or may use magic to secure the arrangement. But murdering the pact-maker is more fun...

WHAT DO DEMONS WANT IN RETURN?

Demons want souls. Souls are food, souls are slaves, souls are currency in the astral plane. Demons rarely accept anything less. Note that this does not have to be the pact-maker's soul, *if* he can get someone else to willingly give theirs to the demon instead.

Sometimes, a demon may accept less than a soul if the pact-maker can aid the demon's goals in another way. A sorcerer might be tasked with assassinating a rival demon, for example, while a normal human might be able to aid the demon by helping it gain revenge on a human who defeated it.

A pact could also be struck for placing a cursed (demon-possessed) object in a holy location, or forming a cult to worship the demon. Typically, demons do less for non-soul payments.

Also, keep in mind the type of demon the pact is being struck with. A terror demon's demands are likely to involve committing violence, while a tempter is likely to request something more subtle and devious —even something that may seem harmless or nonsensical to the pact-maker, but which has far-reaching consequences. A sorcerer demon's demands are likely to involve a quest for rare magical knowledge or spell components, or to aid one of their descendants or blood relations.

Gods and princes demand the most because they offer the most. Void demons are a wild card, offering a lot for what seems like a little, but that "little" is always in the interest of ripping off the seal of their prison. However, they are just as likely to kill or drive insane anyone who contacts them.

WHAT ARE DEMONS LIKE?

It's easy to stereotype demons by rank: familiars are slyly obsequious, terrors are cruel, tempters are charming, sorcerers mysterious, etc. It's also safe to say all demons are arrogant bullies and liars. They're lazy, and despite all their bluster, in the end, most are cowards. But they're more than that.

Each demon is different, just like all people are different. It will have its own personality, interests, and goals, despite whatever limitations the demonic hierarchy puts on it. It is unwise to underestimate them, even worse to provoke them. It's possible to win a few battles fighting fire with fire, but you can't win a war playing by their rules.

Demons respect strength, if nothing else, and a show of force is often enough to drive lesser ones away (at least for a time). However, a show of force may amuse, provoke, or interest stronger demons to accept the challenge. Should it look like the human will win, the higher-ranking demon(s) will flee rather than face defeat or destruction, sacrificing lower-ranking demons to cover their retreat. They will do as much damage as possible before they depart. But that is rarely the end; they are immortal and have plenty of time to plot revenge or wait for the human who beat them to die.

TALKING TO DEMONS

As immortal beings, demons tend to know a lot about many different things. However, demons only tell the truth when compelled, or when the truth will hurt the recipient more than a lie. To gain trust, they offer half-truths, or mix truth with lies.

Tempter demons and above enjoy conversation, using it as a weapon, form of control, or delaying tactic. They may alternate talking in different languages or dialects, using different voices, perhaps even voices pulled from the human's mind—especially the voices of dead loved ones.

Demons freely offer stories, theories, and facts; these may sound good at first but ultimately mean nothing (the "word salad" politicians are famous for). If called out on their deception, they will deny and continue to prevaricate. Should that fail, a quick, cruel change of subject or violent outburst usually puts the demon back on top.

Even if you get a demon to tell the truth, keep in mind that they perceive time differently than we do. They avoid speaking in terms of exact times, let alone days, months, or years. Instead, they prefer to answer, "Soon," "Now," or "Later." These words have different meanings to them, so "Soon" could be a decade in human years, "Now" could mean six minutes or six hours (or tomorrow, or next week), and "Later" could be after you're dead!

It's not easy to get them to express the information you want in human time because:

1. They don't want to be helpful; and
2. it's honestly difficult for them (demons are lazy, remember?).

When speaking to a demon, it will always try to puff itself up, lying about its name, rank, power, where it's been, what it knows, etc. Demons pick grand-sounding names to induce fear and command respect like "Eater of Souls," random names made up of harsh consonants and vowels, or common human names ("John" is a favorite). Why do they do this? *The demon wants to confuse you.*

It also wants to look more powerful than it is so you will take its threats and promises seriously. Sometimes, it wants to trick you into thinking it is a "harmless" ghost or less powerful demon so you will underestimate it or apply the wrong tactics. One thing's for sure: most demons claiming to be gods or princes are not.

DEMONS IN THE ASTRAL PLANE

Demons are most often encountered in the astral plane, lurking like bandits and con-men, waiting to ambush or trick astral travelers. They are not as powerful here as they are in Hell, but far more powerful than on Earth. It is also faster and easier for them to call reinforcements here.

DEMONS ON EARTH

Demons cannot enter the physical world, much less possess anyone, without first being granted permission by humans. The important thing to know is that demons have a different idea of what "permission" means.

If you play with the occult, dare one to appear, mock their existence, or are just a generally unhappy, fearful, or angry person, those all count as "permission" for demons to enter your life, even though you did not specifically say that's what you wanted to have happen! Demons are opportunists and parasites (like astral predators, but more dangerous because of their greater intelligence and power).

Think you're having a good time? Bad news: Drinking and doing drugs lower your psychic defenses. If you're self-medicating to cover fear, pain, or self-hatred, you're a prime candidate for demons.

Once "permission" is given, the first demon will use its summon demon ability to bring more demons to share the fun. It may wait a bit to size up the situation and secure its position, and it may try to trick you by asking if it's okay for it to invite "a few friends" over—

you know, to "help" you. It turns out demons also have a different definition for the words "help" and "friends" as well, and as you can imagine, neither definition is what you want them to be.

DEMONIC POSSESSION

Demons want to experience being in a physical body and to spread evil. Because they are amoral energy beings who don't have to physically live with the consequences of their actions, they freely commit crimes and indulge in risky behavior. A possessed body that is no longer useful to them is quickly abandoned, unless they're magically bound to it.

Demons attempt to gain possession of humans by any means necessary. Terror Demons will not be particularly subtle about it; they may demand it, shouting "Let us in!" or making threats that sound real, but which they may have no actual way of backing up, such as "Let us in or we will kill your daughter!" Never mind that the daughter lives three states away and has no demons anywhere near her. The human will have no way of knowing that!

Should threats not work, terror demons wage psychic war on the intended victim, hoping to wear down their defenses so they can force their way in, or convince the victim to give in. Should that not work, they will resort to violence, again hoping to wear the victim down, but also to punish it.

Tempter demons will be far more subtle in their approach. They are not in a hurry (at least not usually). They use logic, flattery, and lies to establish trust, maybe provide a few private displays of their power, like levitating the victim in an enjoyable manner.

The tempter demon may offer all kinds of benefits and rewards for allowing it to enter the victim. It may present itself as a savior against any terror demons that are plaguing the victim, in the ultimate "good cop, bad cop" routine.

Once the victim agrees to let it in, that's when the tempter demon drops its best friend act and starts torturing the victim, breaking them down to make room for the tempter to have full control. If the tempter goes through its friendly act and the victim still refuses to let it in, the tempter may resort to violence.

Sorcerer demons are less interested in possessing humans. They know what it's like to have a physical body, since they were human once themselves; that aspect holds small appeal because they prefer being energy beings. So they will only possess humans if it suits their goals, using whatever tactics the situation merits, including casting spells.

Sorcerer demons are especially adept at possessing people of their human bloodline, so these tend to be their primary targets. Additionally, bodies they have some genetic connection to feel more like "home" to them.

Gods and princes only possess humans as part of some larger goal. To get their way, they may attempt the friendly seduction of tempters or the psychic war of terrors, but they might cut right to the chase, using cold logic and offering juicy pacts. These are heavy-hitters who don't fool around.

Remember that all demons may possess animals and objects as well as humans. They may also possess an area, say the size of a house or city block. Anything possessed by demons will gradually take on a sinister and oppressive appearance and atmosphere, as well as being at least ten degrees colder than normal. Weather in the area will worsen, plants will wither, and animals will avoid it.

STAGES OF DEMONIC POSSESSION

The first stage is INFESTATION, when you knowingly or unknowingly invite the demon in. The most common forms of infestation are thoughts, dreams, or hallucinations of a frightening or seductive nature. They are most likely to be noticed at three a.m. (the demonic "witching hour"), but may occur at any time and tend to repeat in groups of three or six, which is a calling card of the demonic. Three loud knocks at the door (but no one is there) is an example.

Sudden drops in temperature or chills indicate a demon is physically present, even if it cannot be seen. Demons can drain and manipulate electronic devices (beware dimming lights, phones dying, etc.).

Demons may employ psychokinesis (also known as telekinesis) to cause objects to be lost or found, or to move untouched. They can easily move heavy furniture or appliances, even cars and trucks. The results can be deadly.

The second stage is OPPRESSION (sometimes called "Obsession"), when the demon exerts greater control and influence over its victim and those around it. During this stage, the demon weaves itself more tightly into all aspects of daily life. This is achieved via a combination of psycho-kinesis and telepathy to make itself appear all-knowing and all-powerful.

The third and final stage is POSSESSION, which may be full or partial, voluntary or involuntary. At this point, the victim becomes a host to be used and controlled by the demon. The victim's consciousness may be temporarily displaced or cast out permanently while the demon has ownership of the body. During this time, the possessed may or may not have any memory of what is happening. A "reverse exorcism" may be necessary to return the victim's soul if it has been displaced or cast out of the body.

SYMPTOMS OF DEMONIC POSSESSION

Demons are energy vampires—spiritual parasites that feed on others to sustain their unnatural existence as well as to power a wide range of supernatural abilities. Although they can draw some nourishment from electronic devices, their primary food source is psychic energy, preferably harvested from the negative emotions of living victims. The results of such feeding produce the symptoms of demonic possession.

Such symptoms may be gradual or come on suddenly. They will always include one or more of the following:

- Personality changes including unusual patterns in behavior, emotions, intelligence, morality, or sexuality;

- Physical changes including appearance or voice, dizziness, vomiting, headaches, blackouts, weight loss, paralysis, sleep patterns or sleepwalking, anesthesia to pain or temperature, or signs of abnormal strength or weakness;
- Mental changes including speaking and understanding unknown languages, experiencing delusions and hallucinations (such as hearing voices or seeing things no one else can), paranoia, altered memories or memory loss, exhibiting psychic or occult powers, predicting the future, or otherwise knowing things you could not possibly know;
- Spiritual changes including uncontrollable urges to commit blasphemy or being affected by prayer in an unusual manner, or exhibiting a negative reaction to or fear of holy names and religious objects. However, in the case of an atheist, agnostic, or New Age victim, there may be no such symptoms until an opportunity for religious conflict presents itself.

While anyone could exhibit a few of the less obvious symptoms without being under demonic attack, the more drastic the changes, the greater the likelihood that a demon is involved. An immediate exorcism should be conducted. Note that several exorcisms may be necessary to remove particularly strong demons.

The longer a demon is allowed to remain, the more difficult it is to remove. Nor can a demon ever truly be exorcised unless the possessed actively renounces it and all ties to it. Those who knowingly or secretly enjoy what the demon offers are doomed to remain in its clutches.

HOW TO STOP A DEMON

A demon can be magically forced out of a possessed body or object by a spell or religious ritual, such as the rite of exorcism (which works on ghosts and undead as well). It can be tricked or even convinced to leave as well, though this is obviously not easy.

One terrible tactic amateurs use is inviting the demon to possess them instead. The only demons that will find this an acceptable alternative are the ones capable of possessing multiple humans at the same time: in other words, gods and princes, the worst of the lot!

Because possession is permission-based, the easiest and most effective way to exorcise a demon is for the person it is being possessed by to simply renounce the demon by revoking its invitation and commanding it to leave. This can (and should) be a blanket revocation of all demonic entities present. Such banishment is instantaneous and foolproof, but *only* if the possessed person means it. There can be no doubt, no fear, no secret desire to remain in the demon's thrall. And the act is always draining.

The formerly possessed person will take weeks or months to fully recover, but should feel instantly better, happier, and more like their old self. However, there may be personality changes (for better or worse) as well changes in their spiritual beliefs (an atheist may turn agnostic, for example).

Sometimes, the possessed person will have learned a valuable lesson or truth about themselves from fighting the demon(s) and their life afterward will be far better than before they were possessed. However, this may be impossible to explain, or for others to accept that the person needed to undergo such a grueling experience.

The greatest change is the void left in the victim by the possessing demon's absence; it will ache like a phantom limb. Some part of the person will *miss* being possessed, will miss having the demon's constant companionship and the feeling of psychic power, of forbidden knowledge having been at their fingertips. It's like having an abusive ex-lover, or being a recovering addict. These feelings may take years to go completely away, and until they do, the formerly possessed person is at risk of inviting the demons back...

SAMPLE DEMONS

- *Night of the Demon* (1957, aka *Curse of the Demon*)

- *Rosemary's Baby* (1968)
- *The Dunwich Horror* (1970)
- *The Exorcist* (1973)
- *The Omen* (1976)
- *Suspiria* (1976)
- *Damien: The Omen 2* (1978)
- *The Amityville Horror* (1979)
- *Evil Dead* (1981)
- *Demons* (1985)
- *Angel Heart* (1987)
- *The Gate* (1987)
- *Hellraiser* (1987)
- *Hellbound: Hellraiser 2* (1988)
- *Stephen King's Needful Things* (1993)
- *The Devil's Advocate* (1997)
- *Fallen* (1998)
- *The Ninth Gate* (1999)
- *The Exorcism of Emily Rose* (2005)
- *Supernatural* (TV, 2005-present)
- *End of the Line* (2007)
- *Exorcismus* (2010)
- *The Last Exorcism* (2010)
- *The Shrine* (2010)
- *Asmodexia* (2014)
- *The Babadook* (2014)
- *Devil's Due* (2014)
- *It Follows* (2014)

DEMON PLOT IDEAS

1. A sorcerer seeks to cheat death by making a demonic pact.
2. Teenagers summon a demon through a Ouija board.
3. A family moves into a house possessed by demons.
4. A demon offers to help a lonely teen get revenge on bullies.

5. A woman inherits an old ring possessed by a demon.
6. A serial killer makes a pact with a demon in order to continue killing after he dies.

GHOSTS

Ghosts are a unique type of energy being: human souls, the only kind that has ever truly been alive in a physical sense. Sometimes, these souls become trapped on earth. This can happen for any one of five reasons:

1. The soul doesn't realize it is dead;
2. The soul realizes it is dead, but fears moving on or does not know how;
3. The soul realizes it is dead but has been cursed, tricked, or magically bound to remain;
4. The soul realizes it is dead but has unfinished business to resolve before moving on; or
5. The soul realizes it is dead and wants to live again by possessing the living.

GHOST MOTIVATIONS AND GOALS

Whatever its reasons for remaining, a ghost stubbornly clings to the physical world. Fear, hate, love—any strong emotion can be a source of energy for them.

A ghost is typically bound to the site of its death, but this is not always the case if that site is disturbed, torn down, or moved. Ghosts may attach themselves to portable objects, but more often, they attach to the living, particularly to likeminded individuals, or to friends or family.

Like demons, attached ghosts influence their host subconsciously. Anytime you hear a voice in your head that refers to you in the third person, such as "You want to leave this place," or in a plural sense, as in "We want to leave this place," it may be a ghost, demon, or other spirit trying to influence you. More than one ghost can attach itself to a single person.

Common places to pick up ghost attachments are abandoned buildings, asylums, bars, battlefields, cemeteries, drug dens, and hospitals. Ghosts attach themselves more easily when the living target is afraid, angry, unhappy, sick, inebriated, unconscious, or in an altered mental state.

In some cases, an attached ghost can possess the living. The host's personality is submerged, leaving the ghost in control to do as it wishes. This may be to resume a physical addiction or pursue a goal it left unfinished in life. The host may or may not have any memory of what their body does during this time.

TALKING TO GHOSTS

Ghosts communicate telepathically or through electronic devices. Few are able to adequately mimic physical speech; when they try, it tends to come out as moans and wails, though simple messages can sometimes be conveyed.

The only way ghosts can reliably communicate with the living is by possession. This is typically done through a seance where a willing psychic medium invites the ghost to temporarily possess her to talk to a group or individual.

Such communication is often halting, hissed, and forced, as the ghost is not used to having lungs, drawing breath, and using a mouth to clearly enunciate syllables. Awkward pauses between words or groups of words are common, such as, "You... will leave this place and... never return!"

OBLIVIOUS GHOSTS

Oblivious ghosts are stuck in a time loop. They do not notice or do not care about the living; in most cases, they aren't even aware they're dead. They can be seen by the living only at specific times in specific locations, either going about the tasks they performed in life or repeating the actions that led to their death.

If there is more than one ghost present, they are often related somehow, and one (usually the murderer) will dominate the others. Victim ghosts may attempt to warn the living of the danger, while the murderer ghost may try to add the living to his "collection" of ghosts he can dominate.

FRIENDLY GHOSTS

Friendly ghosts believe they are helping the human they are attached to, and while they may be able to provide short-term benefits of wisdom, comfort, skill, or talent, in the long term, they do more harm than good. They do this by interfering with the human's journey, manipulating their decisions to do the things the ghost thinks they should do.

SELFISH GHOSTS

The most common kind, selfish ghosts are not concerned with their host's well-being, nor do they actively seek their destruction. They simply want to go on doing what they did in life, and the host is taken along for the ride. Selfish ghosts may take actions to protect their host, but only to keep the possession going. A sick or dead host is no good.

HOSTILE GHOSTS

There are two kinds of hostile ghost: hermits and haters. Hermits simply wish to be left alone. As such, they are more concerned with driving the living out of the area they haunt, but will resort to harming those who can't take a hint.

Haters, on the other hand, actively hate the living and *want* to harm them. They don't fire "warning shots" like hermits. In life, they were jealous, vengeful, or insane. Some were or are possessed by demons (yes, ghosts can be possessed!).

Here are three specific kinds of haters:

BANSHEES (HOSTILE GHOST)

A banshee is the ghost of a murdered woman who only appears after dark. Her primary method of communication with the living is an ear-splitting shriek or wail. This warns that someone close is about to die a violent death. Banshees only appear to those who know the upcoming victim. The victim could be the person who hears the wail, or someone nearby (not necessarily within earshot), but there will be some kind of physical limit on how far away the death will occur. A range of five miles is typical because banshees are limited to the general location of their death.

The banshee was the victim of a violent death herself, and is motivated by a strong sense of justice or revenge. Her soul has chosen to remain behind to warn or terrorize others about violent death. For example, a woman murdered by a gang of men may come back to warn other women the same fate is coming for them, or to terrorize the men that they are about to die. Depending on when the banshee is encountered, the death can be immediate, or take place anytime that same night but *before* sunrise.

Certain banshees are murderers themselves (often child-killers), who return not to warn or avenge, but to continue killing, and such deaths may be by drowning or other physical methods. The Mexican legend of *la Llorona* ("the Weeping Woman") is one such case and an apparent exception to the rule of ghosts avoiding water—although drowning someone near the shoreline is different than trying to cross the water. Perhaps some ghosts with a strong connection to water can enter and remain within it up to a point, though this may rapidly deplete their energy.

Variant types of banshee might be able to use their sonic wail to deafen, incapacitate, or kill physical creatures (possibly even physical undead), with gruesome effects like blood running from their ears, eyes, and mouth as the brain and internal organs are vibrated to mush.

Rather than be physically heard, a variant wail might be entirely psychic in nature, but no less devastating (think of the exploding heads from *Scanners*). The added bonus here is that even in a room full of people, only the chosen victim would be able to hear it, making them look sick or crazy.

POLTERGEISTS (HOSTILE GHOST)

A poltergeist is a pseudo-ghost: a "thought golem" created by strong negative emotion that takes on a psychic life of its own. The purpose of that life is to cause harm to a specific individual and those in their immediate vicinity. Only those who attempt to interfere with its purpose (by getting in the way of its attacks on the target) will themselves be attacked.

The poltergeist is psychically attached to the target and cannot be reasoned with, though it can be temporarily tricked or left behind. A poltergeist is insane and can only communicate through imprinting short, horrifying images on its target's brain; images interpreted as "Hate," "Die," "Suffer," etc. These images may include a shadowy figure that represents the poltergeist, and the target may easily misinterpret that figure to be a true ghost or demon.

Poltergeists always remain invisible and focus their energy on causing physical and psychic harm. They can levitate and hurl objects, pinch, bite, hit, trip, even commit sexual assault. However, lacking a true mind, they cannot possess the living. If seen in the ethereal plane, a poltergeist appears as a mad caricature of the person who created it.

If the target of a poltergeist can refrain from feeding it strong negative emotion for a long enough time, the poltergeist will wither and die on its own because unlike ghosts, it can only feed on energy from its target. Also, if the person who created the poltergeist dies, the poltergeist dies.

The Entity (1981) is based on the allegedly true story of a woman who was repeatedly assaulted by a poltergeist.

WRAITHS (HOSTILE GHOST)

Wraiths are created from the corrupt souls of powerful, ambitious murderers whose dreams of conquest and control were cut short. As such, wraiths embody hatred, cruelty, and a desire to dominate and destroy the living. They prefer to do this through physical means.

A wraith's ectoplasm is different from other ghosts. It appears as a billowing gray fog that takes on a humanoid shape. This ectoplasm is more substantial than other ghosts and can be used to "fill up" a suit of clothes or armor to give it a more life-like appearance, at least at a distance. Wraiths easily manipulate physical objects and are rarely found without the signature weapons and armor (or uniform) they loved in life, along with treasured objects such as gold or the bones of their victims.

Unlike ghosts, wraiths are always linked to a single, easily portable object rather than to their physical remains. That object is usually their favorite weapon or armor, but could be anything: a ring, a portrait, a book, etc. Durable, fire-proof objects are generally preferred because destroying the object destroys the wraith.

Wraiths speak in short, hissing whispers when in physical form, but most of their communication is done via telepathy. While they need to feed on psychic energy the same as other ghosts, wraiths are rarely patient enough to hang around haunting for long. Instead, they prefer to quickly inspire terror and despair in their victims, then murder them by their preferred method, harvesting the maximized energy before moving on to the next victim.

Wraiths are bullies, but not cowards. They are sadistic, cunning strategists who enjoy a good fight (though they will retreat rather than be destroyed). Unless united by bonds of blood, a curse, or common cause, wraiths are solitary predators. They are found in battlefields, ruined castles or fortresses, or museums, always close to their linked object.

A variant type of wraith is the *skin wraith*. Rather than fill up armor or uniforms, skin wraiths pour their ectoplasm into a living target to both possess and "armor" them. It reinforces its control by fusing its ectoplasm with the muscles and organs of the host, creating a thin layer of armor that provides protection against damage. When the living host is killed or no longer of value, the skin wraith removes this ectoplasmic connection, billowing out of the host's mouth as a slimy gray fog before vanishing. Some skin wraiths can possess anyone in this manner, others are limited to only possessing people related to them.

GHOSTLY POWERS

All ghosts share the same standard set of strengths and weaknesses. More powerful ghosts have more psychic talents or supernatural powers, and may know a variety of magic spells (if they were a wizard or witch when alive).

STANDARD GHOST PSYCHIC TALENTS

- Astral Projection (once, to escape the ethereal plane)
- Bilocation (Ability to be in the material and ethereal planes at the same time)
- Enhanced Senses (Cannot be surprised, etc.)
- Influence Others (Implant Hypnotic Suggestions)
- Locate Energy Beings and Hide from Same
- Psychokinesis (aka Telekinesis)
- Read Auras
- Telepathy (One-way or two-way)

STANDARD GHOST SUPERNATURAL STRENGTHS

- Create Ectoplasm
- Immortality
- Invisible to Humans
- Levitation

STANDARD GHOST SUPERNATURAL WEAKNESSES

- Cannot Cross Running Water (except by bridge, etc.)
- Hurt by Iron
- Must Feed on Psychic Energy
- Must Rest in Ethereal Plane to Recharge Its Powers
- Repelled by Salt
- Repelled by Water

Like demons and other energy beings, ghosts are invisible to the human eye, but animals can sense their presence and avoid them. Being incorporeal, ghosts can pass through physical barriers like walls, doors, and windows. This includes living things, who will feel a strong chill as the undead passes by or through them.

In fact, that is how most living creatures become aware a ghost is present: the ghost constantly emit a cold sensation, dropping the temperature in a ten- to twenty-foot radius around them by approximately ten degrees. The more powerful the ghost, the larger the radius of the cold. The most powerful ghosts are able to decrease the temperature by another ten or twenty degrees. This may be done by choice, or as an involuntary side effect of having so much power.

Note that ghosts feeding on negative energy can only drop temperatures, but ghosts feeding on positive energy can choose to raise them. For example, to save the life of someone trapped in a car in a snowstorm.

MANIFESTING IN REALITY

It requires a lot of psychic energy for ghosts to manifest themselves in the physical world. Some, like poltergeists, never appear except in victim's minds, while others can take on a semblance of physical form through *ectoplasm*, a viscous substance that is lighter than air and dissolves when the ghost ceases to concentrate on it or runs out of energy. Ectoplasm can present as various shapes, but is most often used to create a humanoid form that resembles how the ghost looked in life. More powerful ghosts can take on other forms, from animals to monsters.

When manifesting in the physical world, ghosts may or may not be bound to the location of their death. They are always motivated by selfish desires (no matter how well-intentioned), so this often translates into becoming extremely territorial. They may want to stay in their house at all costs, for example, or in their town, or the surrounding area. Others relish their newfound freedom to go anywhere. Some choose to follow people they have left behind or grown attached to after death.

Ghosts prefer to manifest after dark, or in darkened areas: attics, basements, forests, underground. It is easier and uses less energy for them to manifest there rather than in sunlight.

THE ETHEREAL PLANE

Ghosts exist in the *ethereal plane*, the so-called "ghost dimension" that overlaps with our planet's magnetic field. The ethereal both powers and is powered by trapped souls.

To those who enter the plane, it appears as a carbon copy of the living world, only darker, duller. There is no sunlight here, only dark gray sky. The plane exists in simultaneous temporal layers that can be peeled like an onion, allowing a form of "spiritual time travel." Thus, some ghosts will only be present and visible in certain layers, though they still manifest in the present to the living. That is because to the ghost, ethereal time can be frozen at the moment of their death. So to a ghost that died in 1979, it is always 1979 if they want it to be, or if they don't know that they are dead.

A living creature cannot physically enter the ethereal plane; they can only enter by leaving their body through astral projection. A living soul in the ethereal may or may not be immediately recognized as such by ghosts, but once recognized, they will be hounded and hunted, whether to ask for help, to possess, or to become psychic food.

Upon death, souls always have enough energy to break through the ethereal plane, to reach "escape velocity" and project themselves into the astral plane, where they will continue their journey to whatever their final destination is. To a ghost, their one-time gate to the astral plane will resemble a door or tunnel of light. Opening it or moving into it immediately sucks them out of the ethereal into the astral—a one-way ticket.

Some souls need time to process the fact they are dead and/or want to make sure those they left behind are going to be okay. But a soul only has enough power to remain in the ethereal for a few days, a week at most, before losing the ability to astral project. After that, they are trapped in the ethereal as ghosts until rescued or captured by other energy beings, or until they feed on enough psychic energy to astral project—but that ability will not be restored for long.

The ethereal plane feeds off ghost energy, though certain powerful ghosts and undead have learned to feed off it. When the plane has drained a soul of enough energy, that soul can no longer manifest itself and falls into a spiritual coma. Eventually, it is consumed.

Note that demons and most other energy beings can move freely and not be trapped by the ethereal plane because it does not recognize their energy as "food." however, aliens whose souls share certain similarities with humans can be trapped. This may explain why some people feel like they have been born into the "wrong world;" to escape the ethereal, these alien souls have chosen to incarnate themselves into a human child. These "star children" think and act differently (perhaps having Asperger's or other odd or autistic traits), but their very difference is what allows them to make great contributions.

On a related note, when new human (or compatible alien) souls come to Earth, they first enter the ethereal plane and begin shadowing expectant mothers in the material. They have sufficient energy at this point to project their soul out of the ethereal into the physical body of a viable fetus.

Should the newly incarnated soul learn the mother is not a good match to carry it to term or raise it to adulthood, it may choose to "abandon ship" and astral project itself back to where it came from, resulting in a miscarriage or stillborn.

Demons cannot enter a fetus without a soul, so they lurk in the ethereal hoping to hitch a ride on a newly arrived soul, or striking bargains with newly dead souls to put them back in a human body (whether a "fresh start" fetus or not).

PSYCHIC ENERGY DRAIN

To prevent being consumed by the ethereal plane, ghosts must feed off the psychic energy of living creatures. That psychic energy comes from manipulating emotions—the stronger, the better. The more energy they feed on, the more power they have, but this is always a limited reserve. Even ghosts capable of tapping into the ethereal itself can only draw so much energy before being destroyed (similar to a tick who pops after gorging on too much blood).

Victims of this psychic drain feel lethargic and apathetic. They are self-absorbed by their relationship with the ghost, whether that relationship is loving or hateful. The more the victims think about the ghost, the more energy the ghost is able to take.

Ghosts feed on either positive or negative emotion; this is determined by personal choice or the type of ghost they are. For example, a friendly ghost who wants to help the living will feed on positive emotions, while a hateful ghost feeds on negative emotions. Drawing nourishment from the opposite energy type initially sickens them, and if they continue to feed on it, it will eventually alter their personality, turning a friendly ghost hateful and a hateful ghost friendly—or at least neutral.

Friendly ghosts, or ghosts who do not realize they are dead, may not understand they are causing more harm than good. Most types of ghosts know they are harmful and either don't care, think the ends justifies the means, or enjoy hurting the living. Some want to kill the living to create more ghosts, either to let them wander in pain or to remain as slaves to terrorize and feed on.

TYPES OF GHOST POSSESSION

Ghost possession can be a total, where the ghost's consciousness dominates the host, or it can be partial, where the ghost only has control of the host for a limited time or under certain conditions. A third type is shared possession, where the undead is inside the host as a kind of "spiritual hitch-hiker." It influences the host to take actions it finds favorable, but cannot force them to comply. Whatever the degree of possession, the host may or may not be aware they are possessed.

One way a host may realize a ghost is sharing its body is to hear thoughts in the third person, such as "You want to drink alcohol," or "We want a drink! Pour us a shot." Since nobody thinks in third person or the plural, this is a clue a ghost is attempting to manipulate them, though they may instead think they are becoming mentally ill.

The ghost's personality, mannerisms, morality, and physical defects tend to manifest in the host either over time or quite suddenly. So for example, a ghost who had a limp when alive would walk with a limp while possessing its host, even if the host's legs were perfectly healthy. If the ghost is foreign, or from another time, the host may develop a strange accent, dialect, speech pattern, or total fluency in the ghost's language. If the ghost of a brilliant college professor possessed a high school dropout with a low I.Q., the host might develop an extraordinary vocabulary and launch into complex conversations, lecturing about topics he could have no way of knowing.

To prevent being discovered, the possessing ghost will try to distance itself from any of its host's friends or family. This distancing will be by the most expedient means possible: by being rude, withdrawn, or angry, by making up excuses, by moving, or even running away.

One more point about possession: The ghost will often, but not always, attempt to return to whatever its goals were in life—unfinished business is the number one reason souls become ghosts. It could be for a short-term goal like to avenge a wrong or make amends, or long-term, from getting drunk and partying every day to running a multinational corporation. Whether or not the goal is practical or not doesn't matter to the ghost. It will be completely delusional and difficult, if not impossible, to reason with regarding its unfinished business. Helping the ghost achieve its goals may be the key to allowing it to move on, or it may bring greater harm to the living.

HOW TO STOP A GHOST

Various ghost-hunting equipment exists; these range from laughable rip-offs to sophisticated sensors that can monitor temperature changes or hear undead talking (see the movie, *White Noise*, for one such example). Ghosts, like energy beings, can interfere with electronic devices, so devices cannot always be trusted to provide accurate information or even to work when you need them.

Weak ghosts can be avoided by keeping calm, giving them no energy to feed on. If a ghost is evil and strong, it can be temporarily repelled by force-feeding it positive emotions. Positive emotions sicken and weaken evil ghosts, who must use up more and more of their negative energy to remain present, let alone fight back. Most will choose to quickly depart rather than risk going into a spiritual coma. They return once their energy levels have been restored.

What about force-feeding a friendly ghost positive emotions? That would have the opposite effect, making it more powerful. This is only advised if the object of feeding it is to give it enough energy to break free of the ethereal plane and continue its spiritual journey in the astral. Even then, they will likely resist the idea (at least at first), insisting they can do more good here. They are afraid of not being able to help the living they leave behind and afraid of being alone in an unknown, possibly hostile environment.

With evil ghosts, it is much harder to convince them they should leave the ethereal. Here, they are big fish in a small pond. *Predators.* They may fear what waits for them in the astral plane and beyond, such as eternal punishment, or becoming prey to more powerful astral energy beings.

Unless possessing the living, ghosts cannot cross a barrier of salt. That's because salt is symbolic of the earth, which is nature, and ghosts are unnatural. Salt also cleanses an area of harmful or negative energies. However, the slightest break in a line of salt will allow a ghost to enter an otherwise protected area.

Iron is considered the life-force of the Earth, its "blood." As such, iron disrupts the energy fields of ghosts, causing them to dematerialize until they can replenish their energy. Carrying a bar or club of iron makes an effective weapon.

Running water also represents life. Unless possessing a living creature or bound into an object, ghosts cannot cross it and must use bridges, boats, or other means of getting across. This means modern underground plumbing systems can trap them, or force them to take the long way around.

Unless stated otherwise, all ghosts are released by convincing them to go to the astral plane, or by salting and burning their bones, or by reducing their bones to ash and scattering them to the wind.

GO HAUNT YOURSELF

One last ghostly idea worth exploring is the concept of reincarnation and past life regression through dreams and hypnosis. This allows a character to effectively "haunt" himself when visions of the past come back to warn or otherwise interfere with his present. Examples include *The Reincarnation of Peter Proud* (1975), and *Dead Again* (1991).

Reincarnation (whether real or misguided) is the basis for many romantic subplots in monster movies, such as *The Mummy* (1932) and *Bram Stoker's Dracula* (1992). After all, if monsters can be real, why can't reincarnation?

What if you were a serial killer in a past life, or a victim? What if you met your killer's reincarnation, or your victim's? Moving beyond the horror genre, what if you were a great hero or villain, but nobody important in this life? How could your past come back to influence you toward glory or infamy? Reincarnation creates a very different kind of ghost story, with new challenges and new opportunities.

SAMPLE GHOSTS

- *The House on Haunted Hill* (1959 and 1999 remake)
- *13 Ghosts* (1960)
- *la Llorona (1960)*
- *The Curse of the Crying Woman* (1961)
- *The Haunting* (1963)
- *The Reincarnate* (1971)
- *The Legend of Hell House* (1973)
- *The Reincarnation of Peter Proud* (1975)
- *Burnt Offerings* (1976)
- *Audrey Rose* (1977)
- *The Changeling* (1980)
- *The Fog* (1980)
- *The Shining* (1980)
- *The Entity* (1981)
- *Ghost Story* (1981)
- *Poltergeist* series (1982-88)
- *Ghostbusters* (1984)
- *A Nightmare on Elm Street* (1984)
- *House* (1986)
- *A Chinese Ghost Story* (1987)
- *Child's Play* (1988)
- *Beetlejuice* (1988)
- *Lady in White* (1988)
- *Shocker* (1989)
- *Ghost* (1990)
- *Dead Again* (1991)
- *Candyman* (1992)
- *Ghost in the Machine* (1993)
- *The Frighteners* (1996)
- *What Dreams May Come* (1998)
- *The Ring* (1999)
- *The Sixth Sense* (1999)

- *Stir of Echoes* (1999)
- *The Others* (2001)
- *The Eye* (2002)
- *The Ring* (2002)
- *Dead End* (2003)
- *The Grudge* (2004)
- *Supernatural* (TV, 2005-present)
- *White Noise* (2005)
- *Pulse* (2006)
- *Paranormal Activity* series (2007-15)
- *White Noise 2: The Light* (2007)
- *Wind Chill* (2007)
- *The Lovely Bones* (2009)
- *Being Human* (TV, 2011-2014)
- *The Woman in Black* (2012)
- *The Conjuring* (2013)
- *Haunter* (2013)
- *Mama* (2013)
- *Last Shift* (2014)
- *The Taking of Deborah Logan* (2014)
- *Unfriended* (2014)
- *Crimson Peak* (2015)
- *Friend Request* (2016)
- *Before I Fall* (2017)
- *Winchester* (2018)

GHOST PLOT IDEAS

1. A struggling author is possessed by a real *ghost* writer.
2. A psychic medium exploits the dead for her own gain.
3. A woman is possessed by the ghosts of her past lives.
4. A woman begs the ghost of her dead lover to stay with her.
5. A lonely man builds a radio to talk to ghosts.
6. A killer's ghost possesses people so he can keep on killing.

FANTASY RACES

HUMANOIDS, MYTHOLOGICAL BEASTS

HUMANOID RACES MAKE UP DWARVES, elves, faeries, gnomes, goblins, orcs, ogres, trolls, and giants. Basically, anything that resembles a human being, but isn't. Many of these can be found in *The Lord of the Rings*, but humanoid races aren't limited to fantasy. For example, *The Creature from the Black Lagoon* (1954) is the last surviving member of an amphibian race of prehistoric "gill-men."

Because these races are not human, they are more complicated to write about. What is their culture like? Their social traditions and sexual conventions? What is offensive or taboo? What does their language sound like? Their music? Their jokes? Their legends? What gods do they worship, if any? Do they have access to different magical, psychic, or supernatural abilities than other races? You won't need to know every detail, but the more you know (even if you don't use them), the better and more realistic they will appear to your readers.

As I advised in Chapter 1: Alien Races, one shortcut is to steal bits and pieces from different real world cultures and then mix those liberally with other influences from movies, books, comics, video games, and TV. You want to be creative, but not *too creative* where your end result is unrecognizable. Fantasy fans will have certain expectations (haughty elves, greedy dwarves, cruel orcs). You want to meet general expectations, but surprise them with a fun twist that makes your version different.

Or, keep the fantasy race traditional, but create a unique individual, an outcast who must struggle to overcome the prejudice of others. Drizzt Do'Urden, a dark elf from the *Dungeons & Dragons* game world, is one of the most famous examples. But you could do the same with any "evil" fantasy race, creating a lone hero or renegade faction. *Hellboy* (2004), a demon turned hero, is another example.

Think about how your humanoid race(s) see the world, and how they view humanity. Are they friends, foes, or neutral? Do they share or compete for resources? Are they persecuted, enslaved, oppressed? Or are they the true masters of their world?

Keep in mind that humans have a bad habit of killing anything that's different from them, and inventing reasons to steal resources that don't belong to them. Look at earth's past. Look at earth's present. Now imagine if we shared the planet with other races that weren't us. Chances are, it wouldn't go well. But then again, maybe it might do us some good to see we're not the only powerful race around. That we'd have to cooperate, have to share. And allies are good to have when something big and nasty shows up.

SAMPLE HUMANOIDS

- *The Creature from the Black Lagoon* (1954)
- *Don't Be Afraid of the Dark* (TV, 1973)
- *The Beastmaster* (1982)
- *Legend* (1985)
- *Labyrinth* (1986)
- *Troll* (1986 and 1990 sequel)
- *The Lord of the Rings* series (2001-03)
- *Hellboy* (2004)
- *Hellboy 2: The Golden Army* (2008)
- *Trollhunter* (2010)
- *Thor: The Dark World* (2013)

- *Warcraft* (2016)
- *The Shape of Water* (2017)

HUMANOID PLOT IDEAS

1. Orcs and humans must team up to face an enemy that wants to destroy them both.
2. An unknown humanoid race is discovered living deep underground or underwater.
3. A human child is stolen and raised by goblins.
4. Humans crush the dwarvish monopoly on gold.
5. Modern day humans open a portal to a "fantasy" world ruled by one or more humanoid races.
6. A humanoid tribe send an ambassador to the humans but he is assassinated, provoking a war.

MYTHOLOGICAL BEASTS

Mythological beasts come in two types: those created by gods from non-human sources, and humans cursed by gods as punishment for their sins. Often, this curse comes with immortality—the beast cannot age past maturity, nor can it commit suicide.

A magical curse can only be broken by the god or creature who placed it, or by fulfilling whatever condition(s) for release were imposed at the time the curse was placed. In some cases, slaying the god or creature who placed the curse can free the victim. Note that "freedom" could mean killing the victim, not returning them to normal. Sometimes, death is mercy.

Some curses only affect the original target, while others can be transferred to a willing or possibly unwilling subject. This may or may not free the original victim of the curse.

A third type of mythic beast is one created not by gods or magic, but by science. Through the science of gene-splicing, all kinds of mythic beasts could be recreated in the lab.

GOALS AND MOTIVATION

Depending on their genetic origin, mythological beasts possess either animal-level intelligence, or human-level intelligence. Those with human I.Q.s have varied goals. They may have resigned themselves to their curse and withdrawn from the world, forging hidden sanctuaries in inhospitable climes where they pursue whatever gives them pleasure: art, books, etc. Or, they could lurk in the shadows, jealous and hating, feeding on the drunk, the weary, the foolish.

Imagine yourself to be immortal but hideous and unfit for society, then add to that a taste for human flesh. You are powerless to avenge your fate on those who bestowed the curse, and you can't stand feeling powerless, so you have to take it out on someone. *Especially someone you can eat.* You are most likely driven by rage, by despair, secretly hoping your next victim will kill you instead.

Or, perhaps you hang on to some twisted semblance of humanity and eat your victims slowly, keeping them alive as long as possible for "companionship." Or maybe you don't eat them but hope to turn them into a monster like you for companionship. Or, you could try to transfer your curse to a willing victim, by playing up the immortality, the power, and leaving out the terrible truth...

VARIANT MYTHOLOGICAL BEASTS

Here's how to give five classic monsters a unique twist:

CENTAURS

Traditionally, centaurs are half-human, half-horse, but there's no reason you can't combine other creatures instead, such as half-human, half-scorpion or half-human, half-spider, or half-human, half-deer. The name "centaur" may need to change as a result, but the half-man, half-beast principle remains the same.

In my coauthored Greek Myth Urban Fantasy series, *The Gods War*, the centaurs are vicious brutes: half-horse, half-ram, half-man.

CHIMERAS

Classically, this is a monster with the body of a goat, the head of a lion, and a serpent's tail. Your chimeras could be a fusion of several fearsome animals or creatures—including humans, as seen in season 5 of *Teen Wolf* (TV, 2015-16).

DRAGONS

Not all dragons breathe fire. Yours could breathe acid, lightning, or nothing at all. You could also make dragon variants that are smaller, wingless, or have barbed scorpion tails. Need inspiration? Check out *Dragonslayer* (1981).

GORGONS

This could be the classical Medusa with snakes for hair and petrifying gaze, or you could create gorgons with snake arms, or the lower half of a snake.

You don't need to limit yourself to serpents; you could use worms, tentacles, whatever you want to create new and interesting "Medusoid" variants. *The Gorgon* (1964) presents a horror spin on the classic Medusa, but for me, the ultimate version was captured in *Clash of the Titans* (1981).

MINOTAURS

This is a man with the head of a bull, but like the Gorgon, you can create all kinds of variants by combining a human with the head of an animal. Why not lion men? Panther women?

Classic minotaurs can be found in *The Chronicles of Narnia: The Lion, the Witch, and the Wardrobe* (2005). Variants can be seen in *The Scorpion King 2* (2008), which features a reptilian one, and *Sinbad and the Eye of the Tiger* (1977), which has a magic-powered robot version.

SAMPLE MYTHOLOGICAL BEASTS

- *The Seventh Voyage of Sinbad* (1958)
- *Jason and the Argonauts* (1963)
- *The Gorgon* (1964)
- *The Golden Voyage of Sinbad* (1973)
- *Sinbad and the Eye of the Tiger* (*1977*)
- *Clash of the Titans* (1981 and 2010 remake)
- *Dragonslayer* (1981)
- *Dragonheart* (1996)
- *The Lion, the Witch, and the Wardrobe* (2005)
- *Minotaur* (2006)
- *The Scorpion King* (2008)
- *Immortals* (2011)
- *Wrath of the Titans* (2012)

CREATURES OF MYTH PLOT IDEAS

1. Your hero goes on a Greek cruise and gets stranded on Medusa's island.
2. An archaeologist unseals an ancient vault releasing a mythic beast into the modern world.
3. People are burned to death after stealing a treasure hoard that belonged to a dragon.
4. When an ancient god is mocked, the disrespectful human is cursed to transform into a mythic beast.
5. A mad scientist uses DNA to recreate a mythic beast that escapes and goes on a rampage.
6. A goat-headed minotaur tricks a modern day witch cult into worshipping it as a demon.
7. An ancient god's curse is transferred to whoever possesses a sacred object from one of its temples.
8. A scientist splices gorgon DNA into his lab assistant.

HUMAN MONSTERS

CANNIBALS, HUMAN FAMILIARS, LIVING ZOMBIES, MANIACS, PSYCHICS, WITCHES

HUMAN MONSTERS COME in all kinds. Your friends, family, neighbors, any of them could harbor some dark secret, some twisted desire...

CANNIBALS

People practice cannibalism for a variety of reasons, usually starvation, but certain indigenous peoples practice it as part of their culture and religion. Some killers practice it as an act of power over victims. But what if there is another option— a supernatural one?

In Algonquian mythology, the Wendigo is an insatiable spirit, a demon of greed, hunger, jealousy, and murder. It is drawn to those who exhibit these dark qualities and attempts to possess them. Once possessed, the Wendigo will rob, murder, and cannibalize humans until the host body is killed. *Ravenous* (1999) is a great example.

SAMPLE CANNIBALS

- *Man from Deep River* (1972)
- *The Texas Chainsaw Massacre* (1974 and 2003 remake)

- *Emanuelle and the Last Cannibals* (1977)
- *Jungle Holocaust* (1977)
- *Antropophagus* (1980)
- *Cannibal Apocalypse* (1980)
- *Cannibal Holocaust* (1980)
- *Eaten Alive!* (1980)
- *Motel Hell* (1980)
- *Cannibal Ferox* (1981, aka *Make Them Die Slowly*)
- *Ravenous* (1999)
- *Fear Itself* (TV, 2008, episode: "Skin and Bones")
- *Donner Pass* (2011)
- *Wendigo* (2011)
- *The Hills Have Eyes* series (2006-07)
- *Wrong Turn* series (2006-14)
- *Cannibal! The Musical* (1993)
- *We Are What We Are* (2010 and 2013 remake)
- *The Colony* (2013)
- *The Green Inferno* (2013)
- *Raw* (2016)

CANNIBAL PLOT IDEAS

1. College kids breakdown and are "helped" by cannibals.
2. A gourmet restaurant is open by invitation only, serving an exclusive clientele of rich cannibals.
3. Nuclear war survivors become sadistic cannibals.
4. The owner of a hotel feeds guests to the cannibal women he keeps locked up in the basement.
5. Modern travelers on the Donner Pass are snowed-in and must resort to cannibalism to survive.
6. A butcher kills people and disposes of the bodies by selling the meat to unsuspecting customers.
7. Mass starvation creates a thriving black market to meet the desperate demand for human flesh.

8. A family of inbred cannibals attack a summer camp.
9. A man gets revenge on his wife and her lover by locking the lover up and forcing him to eat his wife.
10. A cannibal puts an ad in the paper seeking victims.
11. A psychic cannibal eats brains to steal memories.

HUMAN FAMILIARS

Intelligent human villains and monsters (especially undead) will often keep one or more human "familiars" around as a first line of defense and to interface with human society. Think Renfield in *Dracula* (1931), Fritz in *Frankenstein* (1931), Igor in *Young Frankenstein* (1974), Straker in *'Salem's Lot* (1979), and Billy in *Fright Night* (1985).

Where possible, the monster will have a telepathic bond with its human familiar, allowing them to communicate over great distances. This may also extend to the monster having the ability to possess the familiar and act or speak through it. Preferred familiars will be "morally flexible" types who are strong, clever, skilled, and talented in ways the monster finds valuable.

For example, Barlowe and Straker Antiques is the business front used by the vampire, Kurt Barlowe, in Stephen King's *'Salem's Lot*. As the face of the operation, Richard Straker presents himself as a professional antiques dealer, a bit eccentric and stuffy, but not a weirdo. He uses his position to divert suspicion from Barlowe's plans.

But what does Straker get out of the deal, other than a job and a place to live? He gets the benefit of Barlowe's vast fortune to collect the objects he loves with the promise that he will one day be made a vampire as well—that means he can continue to enjoy and add to his collection forever.

Straker also has a few nasty habits of his own that Barlowe lets him indulge. As a result, Straker loves his master. His fear is not of Barlowe himself, but of *disappointing* him. Straker is the perfect familiar: skilled, motivated, ruthless, and utterly devoted to his master.

You could even reason that Norman Bates from *Psycho* (1960) is a kind of human familiar to the split personality of his mother. After all, she's the one who does all the killing, while he has to clean up afterward to "protect" her.

CULTS: WHEN ONE FAMILIAR ISN'T ENOUGH

Without a doubt, the most dangerous type of human familiar are cults that serve a powerful monster, demon, or god, like the villagers in *The Wicker Man* (1973) or *Children of the Corn* (1984).

Sometimes, the "proof" of their god is never seen, as in *Race with the Devil* (1975), but the power of the cult is real, and every bit as dangerous. In this case, the cult could be in service of their leader and ideals rather than an actual supernatural entity. Such cults would resort to regular physical threats and manipulation instead of casting magic spells or summoning demons.

CONSPIRACIES: SECULAR CULTS

Instead of a religious cult, you can substitute secular factions involved in a conspiracy (usually for profit). This could include secret government agencies, wealthy cabals, corrupt legal or law enforcement, etc.

TOP 10 REASONS HUMANS BECOME FAMILIARS

1. To earn the right to become a monster themselves.
2. To have the power of life and death over others.
3. To live nicely on the monster's bank account.
4. To simply be needed, employed, and/or protected.
5. To be part of something bigger than themselves.
6. Out of ambition (the monster has offered to help the familiar succeed at some personal goal).
7. Out of revenge (the monster has promised to help).
8. Out of fear (the monster threatens the familiar's loved ones.
9. Out of love for the monster—what it was, is, or represents.
10. Out of hope the monster will fix the familiar's defects.

SAMPLE HUMAN FAMILIARS

- *Dracula* (1931)
- *Frankenstein* (1931)
- *Bride of Frankenstein* (1935)
- *Son of Frankenstein* (1939)
- *House of Dracula* (1945)
- *Rosemary's Baby* (1968)
- *The Brotherhood of Satan* (1971)
- *Hunchback of the Morgue* (1973)
- *The Wicker Man* (1973)
- *Young Frankenstein* (1974)
- *Race with the Devil* (1975)
- *The Omen* (1976)
- *Damien: The Omen 2* (1978)
- *'Salem's Lot* (1979)
- *Children of the Corn* (1984)
- *Fright Night* (1985)
- *The Believers* (1987)
- *Hellraiser* (1987)
- *Hellbound: Hellraiser 2* (1988)
- *Dagon* (2001)
- *Midnight Meat Train* (2008)
- *The Shrine* (2010)
- *The Following* (TV, 2013-2015)
- *The Ritual* (2017)

HUMAN FAMILIAR PLOT IDEAS

1. A politician's rivals all mysteriously die or disappear.
2. Everyone who bullied a local nerd begins to suffer or die.
3. A loser comes into love or money under odd circumstances.
4. A once-shy outcast begins acting strangely superior.

LIVING ZOMBIES

Living zombies are created through mind control by aliens, hypnosis, magic, mutants, psychics, science, or technology. They are similar to human familiars (particularly cults) but lack free will. Some share a "hive mind" intelligence that allows them to coordinate their actions. They may appear normal, but only if the force controlling them is smart enough to know how to blend into human society.

While in a trance state, living zombies cannot be reasoned with because you are not arguing with the person trapped inside, but with whatever strange and terrible force is controlling them.

Human villains usually create living zombies through drugs and hypnosis, though some also use psychic powers. The most famous examples are *The Cabinet of Dr. Caligari* (1920) and *Svengali* (1931), along with *The Manchurian Candidate* (1962) and *Captain America: The Winter Soldier* (2014).

A subset of living zombies are "regressed" through hypnosis to take on a monstrous physical transformation that may or may not be under control of the hypnotist. Examples include *Blood of Dracula* (1957), *I Was a Teenage Werewolf* (1957), and *The She-Creature* (1956).

Besides working with human familiars, vampires are well-known for creating living zombies out of their hypnotized victims (see the chapter on Undead for more information).

Aliens use mind control to make humans into living zombies in *Invaders from Mars* (1953) and *It Conquered the World* (1956). A variation of the mind control bats used by the alien in *It Conquered the World* are the flying parasites from *Star Trek: The Original Series*, Season One, Episode 29: "Operation: Annihilate!" (TV, 1967).

In Season One, Episode 24 of *Star Trek* (TV, 1967), spores released by weird alien flowers create a tranquilizing effect on the Enterprise crew, effectively making them into "loving" zombies—but despite their happiness, like most zombies, they want to make everyone brainwashed like them.

SAMPLE LIVING ZOMBIES

- *The Cabinet of Dr. Caligari* (1920)
- *Svengali* (1931)
- *Invaders from Mars* (1953 and 1986 remake)
- *It Conquered the World* (1956)
- *The She-Creature* (1956).
- *Blood of Dracula* (1957)
- *I Was a Teenage Werewolf* (1957)
- *The Hypnotic Eye* (1960)
- *Village of the Damned* (1960 and 1995 remake)
- *The Manchurian Candidate* (1962)
- *Children of the Damned* (1964)
- *Star Trek: The Original Series*, Season One, Episode 24: "This Side of Paradise" (TV, 1967)
- *Star Trek: The Original Series*, Season One, Episode 29: "Operation: Annihilate!" (TV, 1967)
- *Empire of the Ants* (1977)
- *The Stuff* (1985)
- *Anguish* (1987)
- *The Brain* (1988)
- *The Puppet Masters* (1994)
- *Slither* (2006)
- *Captain America: The Winter Soldier* (2014)

LIVING ZOMBIE PLOT IDEAS

1. Astronauts come back from space and begin acting oddly.
2. People begin to behave strangely after a UFO is sighted.
3. What appear to be zombies are actually incubators for alien young that burst out of the skull and orifices of their hosts.
4. A mad hypnotist turns patients into his slaves.

MANIACS

Whether they hang out at abandoned summer camps or pricey Manhattan apartments, these "maniacs" are a staple of crime, horror, and thrillers. Some are geniuses, some merely cunning, while others are lumbering morons. Their I.Q. doesn't matter so much as *how* their insanity distorts their thinking and morality.

When portraying mentally ill characters, try to balance your need to tell an entertaining story with your responsibility to accurately depict their illness. This involves research, like discovering "multiple personalities" is now referred to as "dissociative identity disorder."

13 QUESTIONS TO ASK YOUR MANIAC

Like any good psychiatrist, there are a number of important questions you need to ask when creating your maniac:

1. Is the maniac's insanity inherited, the result of a brain injury, drug abuse, torture, a secret government experiment, aliens, or perhaps even the result of a supernatural agency, such as a curse or demonic possession?
2. How does the insanity alter the maniac's thinking?
3. Does the insanity cover a single delusion or many?
4. How does the insanity alter the maniac's morality?
5. How does the insanity alter the maniac's behavior, both on a day-to-day basis and for the long-term?
6. Can the maniac "pass" for normal, and if yes, for how long?
7. If the maniac *cannot* pass for normal, what gives away their insanity and how quickly?
8. Does the maniac operate by some kind of twisted moral code or is he completely amoral?
9. Many maniacs are overconfident of their own abilities. When challenged or confronted, is the maniac more likely to fight, flee, or talk his way out?
10. Does the maniac hear voices, and if yes, how many, and are

they real or part of his insanity? Do the voices have names
and personalities? What are some examples of what the
voices say and how often do they say them?

11. What triggers the maniac to hear the voices, and once
triggered, what is the typical duration the voices are heard?
Is the severity constant or variable?

12. Does the maniac hear any other sounds that *aren't* voices?
What are they? How long do they last? What is the severity?

13. Does the maniac see things that others don't, and are they
real or part of his insanity? What are they? What triggers
him to see these things and how long do the visions last?

SPECIAL PURPOSE

Most maniacs live for a special purpose, from as simple as punishing
sinners to as grandiose as "saving the world" through ritual sacrifice.
This special purpose gives the maniac's tortured life meaning and
keeps him believing that what he is doing is good and important.

Remember, crazy people seldom believe they are mad, and rarely
think of themselves or their actions as evil. They may not like everything they do, but they will do it because they are convinced their
actions are necessary to their own well-being and survival. If there
was no perceived benefit, they would stop.

Think carefully about the reasons your maniac does what he does.
After all, the better you understand him, the better you can write him.

13 QUESTIONS TO ASK YOUR MANIAC

1. What is your maniac's special purpose?

2. How did he decide this was his special purpose and when
did he begin to act on it?

3. How does he pursue this purpose?

4. Does he have a twisted moral code?

5. How does he select his victims?

6. Who is his "perfect" victim?
7. Who will he absolutely refuse to injure or kill?
8. How does he feel each time he completes his special purpose?
9. How often is he compelled to complete his special purpose?
10. Has the maniac ever been caught committing a crime, and if so, by who and when, and what happened as a result?
11. Has the maniac killed before, and if yes, when, who, how, and by what method?
12. Does the maniac feel shame, regret, joy, or nothing over the fate of his victim(s)?
13. Does the maniac have a favorite murder weapon?
14. What other weapons or killing methods does he use, and how proficient is he with them?
15. Is the maniac currently on any sort of medication?
16. Which medications has he tried in the past, and what were the results?

LIMITED TIME MANIACS

A variant of the special purpose is the "limited time maniac," where, for a short period of time, people indulge in psychotic, murderous behavior either willingly (as in *The Purge*), by force (as in *Battle Royale*), or before they disintegrate (as in *Night of the Comet*). Once the limited window to behave without consequence expires (and assuming they are not dead), these maniacs return to their normal behavior.

SAMPLE MANIACS

- *The Lodger* (1944)
- *The Bad Seed* (1956)
- *Peeping Tom* (1960)
- *Psycho* (1960) and *Bates Motel* (TV, 2013-2017)
- *Homicidal* (1961)

- *Whatever Happened to Baby Jane?* (1962)
- *The Sadist* (1963)
- *The Boston Strangler* (1968)
- *Dirty Harry* (1971)
- *Fright* (1971)
- *The Todd Killings* (1971)
- *The Case of the Bloody Iris* (1972)
- *Deliverance* (1972)
- *The Last House on the Left* (1972)
- *The Other* (1972)
- *Silent Night, Bloody Night* (1972)
- *Badlands* (1973)
- *Black Christmas* (1974)
- *Deranged* (1974)
- *The Deadly Tower* (1975)
- *Deep Red* (1975, aka *Profondo Rosso*)
- *Strip Nude for Your Killer* (1975)
- *Alice, Sweet Alice* (1976)
- *Halloween* (1978)
- *The Toolbox Murders* (1978)
- *Beyond the Darkness* (1979)
- *Don't Go in the House* (1979)
- *The Driller Killer* (1979)
- *When a Stranger Calls* (1979)
- *Dressed to Kill* (1980)
- *Fade to Black* (1980)
- *Friday the 13th* series, Parts 1-5 (1980-1985)
- *The House on the Edge of the Park* (1980)
- *Maniac* (1980)
- *New Year's Evil* (1980)
- *The Burning* (1981)
- *Madman* (1981)
- *My Bloody Valentine* (1981 and 2009 remake)
- *The Prowler* (1981)
- *Alone in the Dark* (1982)

- *Pieces* (1982)
- *Slumber Party Massacre* (1982)
- *The House on Sorority Row* (1983)
- *Sleepaway Camp* (1983)
- *The Mutilator* (1984)
- *Silent Night, Deadly Night* (1984)
- *Henry: Portrait of a Serial Killer* (1986)
- *The Hitcher* (1986)
- *Fatal Attraction* (1987)
- *The Stepfather* (1987)
- *Silence of the Lambs* (1991)
- *Single White Female* (1992)
- *The Good Son* (1993)
- *Scream* (1996)
- *Apt Pupil* (1998)
- *Audition* (1999)
- *American Psycho* (2000)
- *Battle Royale* (2000)
- *Ed Gein* (2000)
- *Ted Bundy* (2002)
- *High Tension* (2003)
- *Monster* (2003)
- *The Hillside Strangler* (2004)
- *Saw* series (2004-2010)
- *Hostel* (2005)
- *All the Boys Love Mandy Lane* (2006)
- *Dexter* (TV, 2006-2013)
- *Mr. Brooks* (2007)
- *Inside* (2007)
- *Acolytes* (2008)
- *Martyrs* (2008)
- *The Strangers* (2008)
- *The Loved Ones* (2009)
- *Orphan* (2009)
- *You're Next* (2011)

- *Hannibal* (TV, 2013-15)
- *The Purge* series (2013-present)
- *Tusk* (2014)
- *The Visit* (2015)
- *My Friend Dahmer* (2017)

MANIAC PLOT IDEAS

1. A divorced woman is courted by a charming maniac.
2. A married man has an affair with a a jealous maniac.
3. A summer camp is haunted by a legendary boogeyman.
4. A maniac develops a love/hate obsession with your hero.
5. The hero has a maniac family member out to get him.
6. A maniac targets couples parked in "lovers' lane."
7. Maniacs take over an asylum and pose as the staff.
8. A psycho traps people gathered for the reading of a will.
9. A serial killer is "cured" and released, but is still crazy.
10. An evil hypnotist uses past life regression to turn a patient into a murderer from a past life.
11. An outcast blackmails a serial killer to teach him to kill.

VIRUS MANIACS

Similar to virus zombies (discussed in the Undead chapter), virus maniacs are living maniacs created by a virus, bioweapon, radiation, fungus, or other mind-altering property or substance, such as the modified strain of LSD ingested by drug test patients in *Blue Sunshine* (1977) or the linguistic "word virus" of *Pontypool* (2008).

Virus maniacs may or may not be able to spread their madness through bites and bodily fluids similar to zombies. Depending on the nature and stage of infection, virus maniacs may look perfectly healthy to obviously ill, all the way to horribly diseased and deformed. The effects of the virus may be permanent or may wear off over time or when certain conditions are met (injected with a vaccine, etc.).

SAMPLE VIRUS MANIACS

- *Matango* (1963, aka *Attack of the Mushroom People*)
- *I Drink Your Blood* (1970)
- *The Crazies* (1973 and 2010 remake)
- *Who Can Kill a Child?* (1976)
- *Blue Sunshine* (1977)
- *Rabid* (1977)
- *Cannibal Apocalypse* (1980)
- *The Children* (1980)
- *Nightmare City* (1980)
- *Night of the Comet* (1984)
- *Warning Sign* (1985)
- *Primal Rage* (1988)
- *Grindhouse/Planet Terror* (1997)
- *28 Days Later* (2002)
- *Cabin Fever* (2002)
- *The Happening* (2008)
- *The Signal* (2008)
- *Pontypool* (2009)
- *State of Emergency* (2011)
- *Come Out and Play* (2012)
- *Cooties* (2014)
- *Hidden* (2015)
- *The Girl With All the Gifts* (2016)
- *Viral* (2016)
- *The Cured* (2017)
- *Mayhem* (2017)
- *Mom and Dad* (2017)

VIRUS MANIAC PLOTS

1. A town is targeted for bioweapon testing by the military.

2. A trigger causes cured maniacs to experience a relapse.
3. Certain age groups go crazy (all adults or only kids, etc.).
4. A toxic chemical spill turns people into violent maniacs.

PSYCHICS, WITCHES, AND WIZARDS

Who hasn't wished for magic or psychic powers? The problem is, once you have the ability to cast spells or read minds, you quickly become outside the laws of man and nature. Whether the powers are your own, or borrowed from some alien or supernatural source (such as a god, totem animal, or demon), the uses to which they can be put are limited only by your imagination.

Sources of magic or psychic powers could be:

- Bloodline (one parent was human, the other not)
- Psychic channeling of an alien or supernatural entity
- Genetic mutation or experimentation
- Genie or unknown entity granting wishes (limited in number) such as in Aladdin (1992), Freaky Friday (1976 and 2003 remake), 13 Going on 30 (2004) or Wishmaster (1997).
- Occult and/or Alchemical Study
- Religion (typically in a coven or cult)

SUPERNATURAL AND PSYCHIC POWERS

To create effective magic or psychic powers, put some thought into how you describe them: sights, sounds, smells, tastes, but go beyond the physical into exactly how the user and victims perceive the effects on a mental, emotional, psychic, and/or spiritual level.

Not sure where to begin? Tabletop role-playing games like Call of Cthulhu, Dungeons & Dragons, Pathfinder, and others can be great resources for developing your own magic systems, psychic powers, and spell ideas, even types or "classes" of wizards, such as wizards specializing only in one type of magic. The Alex Verus series of urban fantasy novels by Benedict Jacka do this and are excellent reads.

Psychic powers tend not to be as flashy as magic unless you are talking about the pyrokinesis in *Firestarter* (1984), or psychokinesis (aka telekinesis) in *Carrie* (1976). Your psychic might even be a fraud as in *Seance on a Wet Afternoon* (1964) or begin as one. The antihero in *Shut Eye* (TV, 2016-present) is a total fraud until he gets hit on the head and begins to receive real visions of future events.

For more ideas, refer to Appendix 2: Magic Spells, Appendix 3: Psychic Talents, and Appendix 4: Supernatural Powers.

SAMPLE PSYCHICS

- *Svengali* (1931)
- *Seance on a Wet Afternoon* (1964)
- *Rasputin, the Mad Monk* (1966)
- *The Power* (1968)
- *Carrie* (1976)
- *The Fury* (1978)
- *The Initiation of Sarah* (TV, 1978)
- *Jennifer* (1978)
- *The Medusa Touch* (1978)
- *Patrick* (1978)
- *The Shining* (1980)
- *Scanners* (1981)
- *Poltergeist* (1992)
- *The Sender* (1982)
- *The Dead Zone* (1983)
- *Firestarter* (1984)
- *Aenigma* (1987)
- *Green Mile* (1999)
- *The Sixth Sense* (1999)
- *X-Men* (2000)
- *From Hell* (2001)
- *The Dead Zone* (TV, 2002-07)
- *Next* (2007)

- *Midnight Special* (2016)
- *Shut Eye* (TV, 2016-present)
- *Logan* (2017)

PSYCHIC PLOT IDEAS

1. A government projects recruits or creates psychics to help commit acts of psychic spying and espionage.
2. A man is shot in the head and gains psychic powers.
3. A psychic gets involved in a kidnapping or serial killer case.

SAMPLE WITCHES AND WIZARDS

- *The Wizard of Oz* (1939)
- *Black Sunday (1960)*
- *Burn, Witch, Burn (1962)*
- *The Haunted Palace* (1963)
- *The Raven* (1963)
- *The Witches* (1966)
- *The Devil Rides Out* (1968)
- *Rosemary's Baby* (1968)
- *Witchfinder General* (1968, aka *The Conqueror Worm*)
- *Crowhaven Farm* (TV, 1970)
- *The Dunwich Horror* (1970)
- *Black Noon* (TV, 1971)
- *Blood on Satan's Claw* (1971)
- *The Mephisto Waltz* (1971)
- *Simon, King of the Witches* (1971)
- *Season of the Witch* (1972)
- *Virgin Witch* (1972)
- *Horror Rises from the Tomb* (1973)
- *Satan's School for Girls* (TV, 1973)
- *Spectre* (1977)

- *The Dark Secret of Harvest Home* (TV miniseries (1978)
- *Inquisition* (1978)
- *The Legacy* (1978)
- *Summer of Fear* (TV, 1978)
- *The Beastmaster* (1982)
- *Conan the Barbarian* (1982)
- *The Sword and the Sorcerer* (1982)
- *Angel Heart* (1987)
- *The Believers* (1987)
- *The Witches of Eastwick* (1987)
- *Warlock* (1989)
- *Hocus Pocus* (1993)
- *The Craft* (1996)
- *Little Witches* (1996)
- *Wishmaster* series (1997-2002)
- *Charmed* (TV, 1998-2006)
- *Harry Potter* series (2001-11)
- *The Lord of the Rings* series (2001-03)
- *The Woods* (2006)
- *Season of the Witch* (2011, unrelated to 1972 film)
- *The Secret Circle* (TV, 2011-12)
- *Hansel and Gretel: Witch Hunters* (2013)
- *Salem* (TV, 2014-17)
- *The Witch* (2015)
- *Blair Witch* (2016)
- *Dr. Strange* (2016)
- *Wish Upon* (2017)

WITCH AND WIZARD PLOT IDEAS

1. A witch's ghost wants to possess her descendant.
2. An outcast finds a wizard's spell book to get revenge.
3. A cult wants to open an astral gate to its demon god.
4. A hero's wish is granted in an unexpected way.

6

MACHINES

ANDROIDS, CYBORGS, POSSESSED MACHINES AND MANIAC DRIVERS, ROBOTS, VIRTUAL REALITY NIGHTMARES

ANDROIDS

ANDROIDS ARE robots with a human-like appearance. They may be virtually indistinguishable from humans or built with one or more characteristics that identify them as robots. Androids are equipped with artificial intelligence and programmed to act in ways similar to humans. Due to their human-like appearance and behavior, androids make ideal companions, assassins, and spies.

Depending on their programming, androids may, over time, become obsessed with learning how to become more human (if treated well) or less human (if treated badly). The complicated web of human emotions are the primary stumbling block for androids. They are programmed to mimic emotions, but cannot actually *feel* them. The quest to truly feel and understand emotions is what drive many androids' character arcs.

Another option is for humans to insert themselves into android bodies, either temporarily, or permanently, perhaps as a way to live forever. What kind of android body and attributes would you want if you could remake yourself from scratch? The sky's the limit, or at least your bank account. Check out *Surrogates* (2009) for more on that.

SAMPLE ANDROIDS

- *Westworld* (1973 and 2016-present TV remake)
- *The Stepford Wives* (1975)
- *Alien* (1979)
- *Android* (1982)
- *Halloween III: Season of the Witch* (1982)
- *The Terminator* (1984)
- *Blade Runner* (1982)
- *Aliens* (1986)
- *Star Trek: The Next Generation* (TV, 1987-1992)
- *Terminator 2: Judgment Day* (1991)
- *Screamers* (1995)
- *A.I. Artificial Intelligence* (2001)
- *Imposter* (2001)
- *Surrogates* (2009)
- *Ex Machina* (2014)
- *Chappie* (2015)
- *Humans* (TV, 2015-present)
- *Blade Runner 2049* (2017)

ANDROID PLOT IDEAS

1. Androids are banned; the last remaining ones struggle to hide within the human population.
2. Humans are exterminated by androids and the last remaining humans pose as androids to survive.
3. Androids are used by a foreign power to secretly replace our politicians and business executives.
4. An android learns how to feel and attempts to teach other androids what it has learned.
5. An android learns how to feel but when this leads to tragedy, it tries and fails to shut off its emotions.

CYBORGS

A cyborg is a human or other creature whose physical abilities have been enhanced beyond its natural limits by artificial replacements or modifications. These cybernetic parts may or may not be noticeable; they could be covered with synthetic skin, for example. In humans, the more organic parts that are replaced, the more anger, depression, and mental illness the cyborg may have, as he feels "more machine than man." *Robocop* (1987), dealt with this struggle.

The cyborg theme is one of self-acceptance and identity: If you're not who you were, who are you now? Man? Machine? Something more? Something less?

How are cyborgs treated in your story world? Are they primarily wounded veterans and accident victims, or do people seek out such procedures? Why? Is this for a job, military service, a fetish, or personal fulfillment?

CYBERPUNK CYBORGS

When you think of cyborgs, you may see a picture of someone who is half-man and half-machine, but there is another type of cyborg popularized in cyberpunk films and fiction like *Johnny Mnemonic* (1995). These cyborgs have cybernetic implants in their skulls— data ports they can use to download memories, information, languages, or specialized skills as a shortcut to traditional forms of learning. What if you could instantly become a master of anything you want? Think of the potential for education, careers, and espionage!

CYBORGS EXIST NOW

Cyborgs do not belong solely to the realm of science fiction. People with electronic artificial limbs are the most noticeable, but technically, any wearable or implanted electronic or prosthetic device is cybernetic; this includes pacemakers, hearing aids, and contact lenses.

What would happen if a mad scientist or enterprising criminal could hijack these devices?

For example, sending subliminal suggestions through a hearing aid to brainwash a victim? Or blackmailing a man to commit a crime for him or else his pacemaker will be turned off? Or remote controlling a man's cybernetic arm to strangle someone to death? The possibilities are endless!

CYBORG VULNERABILTY

Cyborgs are vulnerable to EMP (electro-magnetic pulse) effects that can cause unshielded implants to go dead. Depending on what these implants control, this can be a mere nuisance or absolutely crippling.

SAMPLE CYBORGS

There are plenty of cyborgs to be inspired by, from Darth Vader to the Daleks and Cybermen of *Dr. Who*:

- *Dr. Who and the Daleks* (1965)
- *Daleks' Invasion Earth 2150 A.D.* (1966)
- *Star Wars* (1977)
- *The Six Million Dollar Man* (TV, 1974-78)
- *The Bionic Woman* (TV, 1976-78)
- *Robocop* (1987)
- *Cyborg* (1989)
- *Tetsuo, the Iron Man* (1989)
- *Ghost in the Shell* (1995 anime and 2017 live-action remake)
- *Johnny Mnemonic* (1995)
- *Star Trek: First Contact* (1996)
- *Teen Titans* (TV, 2003-06)
- *Iron Man* (2008)
- *Captain America: The Winter Soldier* (2014)
- *Justice League* (2017)
- *Upgrade* (2018)

CYBORG PLOT IDEAS

1. A soldier is saved from death by cybernetic implants but struggles to cope with his new identity.
2. A grieving man undergoes cybernetic surgery to live an isolated life in a harsh environment.
3. A mad scientist seizes control of all the cyborgs and uses them to enact his revenge.
4. A woman gets a cybernetic hearing aid and picks up messages from outer space or another dimension.
5. A foreign power releases cybernetic data chips that download computer viruses into user's brains.

POSSESSED MACHINES AND MANIAC DRIVERS

Demons and ghosts can attach themselves to objects as easily as they can to people, and even alien energy beings or psychic forces can invisibly operate machines to attack us.

Of course, it's more likely there's a maniac human behind the wheel, as in films like *Duel* (1971), *Death Proof* (2007) and the *Mad Max* series (1979-2015). I include maniac drivers here as the focus of these stories is not on the maniac so much as his vehicle.

SAMPLE POSSESSED MACHINES AND MANIAC DRIVERS

- *Duel* (TV, 1971)
- *The Cars That Ate Paris* (1974)
- *The Car* (1977)
- *Death Car on the Freeway* (1979)
- *Christine* (1983 and 1997 remake *Trucks*)
- *Mad Max* (1979)
- *The Hearse* (1980)

- *The Road Warrior* (1981)
- *Nightmares* (1983)
- *Mad Max: Beyond Thunderdome* (1985)
- *Maximum Overdrive* (1986)
- *The Wraith* (1986)
- *Wheels of Terror* (TV, 1990)
- *The Mangler* (1995)
- *Jeepers Creepers* (2001)
- *Joy Ride* series (2001-2014)
- *Black Cadillac* (2003)
- *Highwaymen* (2004)
- *Death Proof* (2007)
- *Hush* (2008)
- *Shuttle* (2008)
- *Phantom Racer* (2009)
- *Road Kill* (2010)
- *Super Hybrid* (2010)
- *Mad Max: Fury Road* (2015)

POSSESSED MACHINES AND MANIAC DRIVER PLOT IDEAS

1. A demon possesses a classic car and whoever owns it.
2. A maniac trucker torments travelers on a deserted highway.
3. A creepy hearse follows people and tries to kill them.

ROBOTS

Robots are autonomous or semi-autonomous machines programmed to carry out complex actions. They may or may not have a human- or animal-like appearance, and may be any size, and mobile or stationary. Robots can be used in hazardous situations and hostile environments without endangering human life. They can also maximize production efficiency in factories.

Replacing humans, while having obvious benefits, breeds anger and anti-robot sentiment in the humans who were replaced. Many humans fear not only job loss to robots, but what happens if robots become sentient and decide to exterminate humanity.

The ethical use of robots and what governs their behavior is also in question. Can robots achieve self-awareness through artificial intelligence, and if they can, are they entitled to the same rights exercised by humans? If not, aren't they our slaves? And what if the robots refuse to accept our decision? What if they choose to enslave or destroy us?

There are many examples of military, industrial, and commercial robots in use or being developed today, from drones to vacuum cleaners to self-driving vehicles and space probes.

NANOBOTS

Nanobots are a new type of robot to watch out for. They are bacteria-sized robots that can be injected into people to perform surgery or into machines to repair them, but they can also be used as weapons. They could assassinate enemies, cripple computer systems, and wreak all kinds of havoc. Some speculate nanobots could cover the earth, devouring everything and turning the planet into "gray goo."

SAMPLE ROBOTS

Need more inspiration? Check out these famous robots:

- *The Phantom Creeps* (1939)
- *Gog* (1954)
- *Forbidden Planet* (1956)
- *Kronos* (1957)
- *Lost in Space* (TV, 1965-1968)
- *Demon Seed* (1977)
- *Star Wars* (1977)
- *Battlestar Galactica* (TV, 1978-79)

- *The Black Hole* (1979)
- *Saturn 3* (1980)
- *The Transformers* (TV, 1984-1987)
- *Voltron, Defender of the Universe* (TV, 1984-85)
- *Robotech* (TV, 1985)
- *Chopping Mall* (1986)
- *Short Circuit* (1986)
- *Robocop* (1987)
- *Robot Jox* (1989)
- *Hardware* (1990)
- *The Iron Giant* (1999)
- *Pacific Rim* (2013)
- *Robot Overlords* (2014)
- *Rogue One* (2016)
- *Solo* (2018)

ROBOT PLOT IDEAS

1. Workers rebel, sabotaging their factory after being replaced by machines.
2. A foreign power introduces a computer virus into their enemy's robot soldiers.
3. A dying scientist transfers his consciousness into the brain of a robot.
4. A race of sentient, self-replicating robots attempts to eradicate humanity.
5. Robots enslave humans, implanting emotion-blocking chips in their brains.

VIRTUAL REALITY NIGHTMARES

Virtual reality can be a monster in and of itself, and it only becomes more fascinating and frightening as technology continues to advance.

There is ample opportunity to explore all kinds of genres and stories in the context of virtual reality.

There is another option instead of going into another reality... What if that other reality can cross over into our reality? This can be as simple as fighting real video game villains like in the legendary "Bishop of Battle" story from the the 1983 horror anthology, *Nightmares*, or it can be as complex as you want. Would these digital people have rights in our world? What if they came into our reality to play us by taking possession of our lives, our identities? And what if we went into their world and became them in the bargain?

What if we aren't real and neither is our world? What if we are the avatars of humans or aliens playing us? Do we go to sleep when they log off? how would we know? What would we do if we discovered the truth?

If you're familiar with the recent blockbuster novel and film, *Ready Player One*, then you know the new genre of LitRPG ("Literary Role-Playing Game") and GameLit is growing in popularity. It features stories of everyday people—gamers like you or me—willingly or unwittingly entering into virtual or real game worlds.

What would you do if you found out you could disconnect from your boring existence and recreate yourself to be as perfect as you want to be—and as powerful—in a game world? How you would you distribute your ability score points? Would you prioritize physical, mental, or social skills? Would you want to be a great warrior, wizard, or rogue? What if you could be any race, any gender, or not even human? What if the only limits to what you could be were your imagination and your character level?

Like it or not, these choices are coming, and it's only a matter of time until we all get to decide who we are from scratch, maybe forever. And maybe we can keep reinventing ourselves, switching bodies, skills, whatever we want. What kind of world will that be, and why would we ever want to leave it?

For ideas about what kinds of game worlds you can create, check out the vast variety of MMORPGs ("Massively Multiplayer Online Roleplaying Games") available.

EXPLORING DREAMS AND THE MINDS OF OTHERS

An alternative to going into a computer-generated digital reality is to harness technology to go *inside the mind of another human.* Imagine what you could learn, what you could do, and what are the ethics of it? Could you alter or influence their dreams, their memories, or only observe? Or could you take over their mind and become them, effectively creating a new reality for yourself?

Entering the minds and dreams of others is explored in films like *Brainstorm* (1983), *Dreamscape* (1984), and *Inception* (2010).

SAMPLE VIRTUAL REALITY NIGHTMARES

- *Tron* (1982)
- *Brainstorm* (1983)
- *Nightmares* (1983)
- *Videodrome* (1983)
- *Dreamscape* (1984)
- *Total Recall* (1990)
- *The Lawnmower Man* (1992)
- *Brainscan* (1994)
- *Strange Days* (1995)
- *Virtuosity* (1995)
- *Dark City* (1998)
- *eXistenZ* (1999)
- *The Matrix* (1999)
- *The Thirteenth Floor* (1999)
- *The Cell* (2000)
- *Vanilla Sky* (2001)
- *Gamer* (2009)
- *Inception* (2010)
- *Tron: Legacy* (2010)
- *Transcendence* (2014)
- *Ready Player One* (2018)

SAMPLE VIRTUAL REALITY NIGHTMARE PLOTS

1. Virtual reality communities open for the rich; anyone with money can have their physical bodies looked after while they enjoy a full- or near full-time virtual existence. What could go wrong?
2. A virtual reality contest gives both real and virtual prizes leading to intrigue, battles, and murders between players.
3. People are able to upload their consciousness to an avatar in virtual reality and become part of their favorite game forever, but their body dies. Your hero faces the hard choice of staying in our reality or moving into another. Who will he leave behind? What will he miss?
4. Someone who died after uploading his consciousness to virtual reality comes back into physical reality through electronic devices to warn or harm with the living both inside and outside the game.
5. A foreign assassin or terrorist downloads his brain into a virtual reality game to steal secrets and/or kill his government or religion's enemies while they are playing the game.
6. In the future, criminals are punished in virtual reality prisons, and given opportunities to role-play their way back to reality by making correct choices. But a system used to correct behavior can also be used to *corrupt* behavior. Naturally, someone has created a program to create the perfect criminals!
7. A fatal attraction cyberstalker downloads her consciousness into your hero's brain so they can be "together forever," or maybe she uploads his consciousness into a private server where he will be trapped with her forever.
8. A serial killer uploads his consciousness into virtual reality to escape justice; he then terrorizes PVP zones, continuing his old murderous habits in a new disguise.

7

MUTANTS

MUTANTS ARE NATURALLY OCCURRING or the product of magical or scientific experimentation. Depending on the mutation, they represent an evolutionary leap forward or backward.

Think about the environment of your story world. Has there been a dramatic change that demands species adapt or die? Have mutagenic chemicals or radiation been released? What effect are they having? Is it a slow change, or sudden? In *Damnation Alley* (1977), within a few years of a nuclear war, scorpions grow as large as dogs and cockroaches scour cities in swarms, feeding on human flesh.

Of course, with magic or science, there's no need for the world to change. There only needs to be the *desire* of the wizard or scientist to create mutations. Is that desire benevolent or malevolent? Brilliant or misguided? Can the mutants be controlled or will they turn on their creator and escape? And what happens when they breed in the wild?

The earliest examples of mutants include *Freaks* and *The Island of Lost Souls* (both 1932). The first film explored the lives of real life sideshow carnival freaks. The second dealt with a mad scientist's attempt to make animals more like humans (with predictably disastrous results). This idea was later adapted as *The Twilight People* (1972) and twice as *The Island of Dr. Moreau* (1977/1996).

The next wave of mutants came in the 1950s-60s with nuclear radiation causing outbreaks of giant bugs, lizards, and even people! In the 1970s-80s, the cause changed to pollution and toxic waste. Since then, DNA tampering and gene splicing has become the number one cause of mutations. Notice how the monsters stay pretty much the same, but the reason for them keeps changing? That's because science scares people, and what we don't understand, we fear.

MUTANTS MAKING MUTANTS

Another idea is mutant parasites that enter a host organism, changing it from within. The David Cronenberg "body horror" film, *Shivers* (1975) features a parasite that stimulates its host's sexual impulses. Unfortunately, the parasite *overstimulates* the host, turning them into violent, sex-crazed zombies.

It doesn't have to be parasites that transform people or wildlife, it could be a virus or toxic waste. In *Mutants* (2009), the virus acts like it does in a zombie movie, and those it infects mutate into subhuman cannibals. In *C.H.U.D.* and *Mutant* (both 1984), exposure to toxic waste turns people into cannibalistic monsters.

SUPERHEROES AND SUPERVILLAINS

Mutants have long been popular as heroes and villains in comic books. People long for extraordinary powers, and depending on what kind of person they are, they could use those powers for good, evil, or selfish reasons. The most realistic depiction of what would happen when people gain super powers can be seen in *Chronicle* (2012).

The source of your story's superpowers could be aliens, government experiments, radiation, whatever you can imagine.

SAMPLE MUTANTS

- *Freaks* (1932)

- *The Island of Lost Souls* (1932)
- *Godzilla* (1954)
- *Them!* (1954)
- *This Island Earth* (1955)
- *Tarantula!* (1955)
- *The Amazing Colossal Man* (1957)
- *Attack of the Crab Monsters* (1957)
- *The Incredible Shrinking Man* (1957)
- *Attack of the 50 Foot Woman* (1958)
- *The Fly* (1958 and 1986 remake)
- *The Alligator People* (1959)
- *The Flesh Eaters* (1964)
- *Octaman* (1971)
- *The Twilight People* (1972)
- *Invasion of the Bee Girls* (1973)
- *Sssssss* (1973)
- *The Mutations* (1974)
- *Bug* (1975)
- *Shivers* (1975, aka *They Came from Within*)
- *The Food of the Gods* (1976)
- *Damnation Alley* (1977)
- *Empire of the Ants* (1977)
- *The Island of Dr. Moreau* (1977 and 1996 remake)
- *The Man from Atlantis* (TV, 1977-78)
- *The Incredible Hulk* (TV, 1978-82)
- *Piranha* (1978)
- *Spawn of the Slithis* (1978)
- *The Brood* (1979)
- *Alligator* (1980)
- *Humanoids from the Deep* (1980)
- *The Funhouse* (1981)
- *Piranha Part 2: The Spawning* (1981)
- *Basket Case* (1982)
- *C.H.U.D.* (1984)
- *Mutant* (1984)

- *The Toxic Avenger* (1985)
- *The Fly 2* (1989)
- *Total Recall* (1990)
- *Mimic* (1997)
- *Bats* (1999)
- *Deep Blue Sea* (1999)
- *X-Men* (2000)
- *Spider-Man* (2002)
- *The Cave* (2005)
- *The Hills Have Eyes* series (2006-07)
- *Wrong Turn* series (2006-14)
- *Splinter* (2008)
- *Mutants* (2009)
- *Splice* (2009)
- *Captain America: The First Avenger* (2011)
- *Chronicle* (2012)
- *Deadpool* (2016)
- *Logan* (2017)
- *Deadpool 2* (2018)

MUTANT PLOT IDEAS

1. The military creates "super soldiers" to fight its wars.
2. A mutagenic virus grants superpowers, but at what cost?
3. Weaponized mutants escape from a government lab.
4. Homeless people sealed in forgotten subway tunnels mutate into cannibals who can see in the dark.
5. Illegally dumped toxic waste mutates the local human and animal population into insane killers.
6. Inbred rednecks mutate into deformed cannibals.
7. A mad scientist splices the genes of humans with animals to create a race of mutant "manimals."
8. Astronauts exposed to an alien parasite mutate into half-human, half-aliens.

SHAPESHIFTERS

CURSED AND NATURAL SHAPESHIFTERS

CURSED SHAPESHIFTERS

Cursed shapeshifters (also known as were-creatures) are humans bitten or otherwise infected by a natural or cursed shapeshifter; they can only take on the same form as the type of shapeshifter that infected them. Unlike natural shapeshifters, they are forced to change on the night of the full moon and possibly at other times (when angry, ecstatic, or injured being the most likely).

A cursed shapeshifter initially has little to no control over their transformation. Control can be learned over time or taught by another shapeshifter, but cursed shapeshifters will never have complete mastery of the process. Maintaining a hybrid form (such as a bipedal werewolf) is possible to achieve with practice—or may be the only type of form a cursed shapeshifter can take; this option is entirely at your discretion.

Where natural shapeshifters flow easily in and out of their forms, cursed transformations tend to be slow and excruciatingly painful. Duration and pain levels can lessen with experience, but they call this a curse for a reason: it's always going to be painful and inconvenient.

It's not uncommon for were-creatures to develop enhanced animal senses permanently in their human form; however those senses will not be as good as when they have transformed.

Although werewolves (lycanthropes) are by far the most common and popular type of cursed shapeshifter, in theory, any type of predatory animal, bird, fish, or insect can be a were-creature. Keep in mind that a werewolf is going to behave differently than a were-spider or were-shark.

Regardless of the type of creature, it is always going to be aggressive and emotionally volatile. It may or may not recognize people it knows in its were-form, and even if it does recognize them, that is no guarantee to prevent an attack. However it can be enough to cause the were-creature to hesitate, flee, or choose a different target.

As predators, cursed shapeshifters are driven by an overwhelming urge to hunt and kill anything they can eat, including humans. Like a spiritual virus, the curse also seeks to propagate itself by causing the were-creature to infect others.

A cursed shapeshifter's human consciousness is likely to blackout during the transformation process and may have no memory (or only scattered nightmare-like flashbacks) of what it did in were-form. Waking up in a strange place naked or in torn clothes, and covered in blood are common ways to suspect you have been cursed. Of course, you could also think you're simply going insane, which is what most people in the modern world will think.

The process of discovery of your true, cursed nature is the focus of most were-creature stories. Some will try to beat the curse, some kill themselves in despair, while others learn to accept (even enjoy) it. Which option will your hero pick?

VARIANT: SCIENCE-BASED SHAPESHIFTERS

Who needs magic when science can replicate the curse? In *Dr. Jekyll and Mr. Hyde* (1931), a mild-mannered doctor invents a potion intended to purge mankind of its evil impulses; instead, his serum creates a split personality: one good, the other a crude physical embodiment of evil. *Dr. Jekyll and Sister Hyde* (1971) takes it a step further by having the doctor transform himself into a beautiful psychotic female instead.

In *The Werewolf* (1956), a mad scientist injects a man with "irradiated wolf's blood" that turns him into a werewolf. Rather than potions or injections, *I Was a Teenage Werewolf* (1957) uses an evil hypnotist to regress a troubled teen to his "primitive state;" the end result being he turns into a werewolf.

In *Monster on the Campus* (1958), a well-meaning scientist accidentally exposes himself to irradiated prehistoric blood; it devolves him into a homicidal caveman.

Yet another example is *The Fly* (1986). In this film, a teleportation accident splices a scientist's DNA with that of a fly; the scientist slowly transforms into a hybrid monster.

SAMPLE CURSED SHAPESHIFTERS

- *Dr. Jekyll and Mr. Hyde* (1931 and 1941 remake)
- *Werewolf of London* (1935)
- *The Wolfman* (1941 and 2010 remake)
- *The Undying Monster* (1942)
- *Frankenstein Meets the Wolf Man* (1943)
- *The Return of the Vampire* (1943)
- *House of Frankenstein* (1944)
- *House of Dracula* (1945)
- *Abbott and Costello Meet Frankenstein* (1948)
- *Abbott and Costello Meet Dr. Jekyll and Mr. Hyde* (1953)
- *The Werewolf* (1956)
- *Blood of Dracula* (1957)
- *I Was a Teenage Werewolf* (1957)
- *The Fly* (1958 and 1986 remake)
- *Monster on the Campus* (1958)
- *The Wasp Woman* (1959)
- *Curse of the Werewolf* (1961)
- *Werewolf in a Girl's Dormitory* (1961)

- *The Reptile* (1966)
- *Mark of the Wolfman* (1967)
- *Frankenstein's Bloody Terror* (1968)
- *The Strange Case of Dr. Jekyll and Mr. Hyde* (TV, 1968)
- *Dr. Jekyll and Sister Hyde* (1971)
- *The Werewolf vs. the Vampire Woman* (1971)
- *Werewolves on Wheels* (1971)
- *Dr. Jekyll Meets the Werewolf* (1972)
- *The Fury of the Wolfman* (1972)
- *Moon of the Wolf* (TV, 1972)
- *The Boy Who Cried Werewolf* (1973)
- *The Cat Creature* (1973)
- *Curse of the Devil* (1973)
- *The Beast Must Die* (1974)
- *Legend of the Werewolf* (1975)
- *Night of the Howling Beast* (1975)
- *Werewolf Woman* (1976)
- *Curse of the Black Widow* (TV, 1977)
- *An American Werewolf in London* (1981)
- *The Howling* (1981)
- *Night of the Werewolf* (1981)
- *The Company of Wolves* (1984)
- *Silver Bullet* (1985)
- *Teen Wolf* (1985)
- *Werewolf* (TV, 1987-1988)
- *Lair of the White Worm* (1988)
- *The Fly 2* (1989)
- *Wolf* (1994)
- *Bad Moon* (1996)
- *Ginger Snaps* (2000)
- *Dog Soldiers* (2002)
- *Ginger Snaps Back: The Beginning* (2004)
- *Cursed* (2005)
- *Skinwalkers* (2006)
- *Jekyll* (TV miniseries, 2007)

- *Never Cry Werewolf* (TV, 2008)
- *Bad Moon Rising* (2011)
- *Being Human* (TV, 2011-2014)
- *The Howling Reborn* (2011)
- *Wer* (2013)
- *Hemlock Grove* (TV, 2013-15)
- *Late Phases* (2014)
- *Teen Wolf* (TV, 2011-17)
- *Penny Dreadful* (TV, 2014-16)
- *Howl* (2015)

CURSED SHAPESHIFTER PLOT IDEAS

1. A necklace originally owned by an Egyptian priestess of Bast curses the wearer to become a cat monster.
2. A big game hunter kills a totem animal on safari and is cursed to become a were-creature of its kind.
3. A troubled teen uses a black magic ritual she finds online to become a were-creature.
4. A hunter is bitten by what he thinks is a wolf...
5. A were-creature is behind mysterious livestock mutilations.

NATURAL SHAPESHIFTERS

Natural shapeshifters (also known as shifters) were born that way or acquired their powers later in life by supernatural means. Some come from earth, some from outer space or other dimensions. Most have only three forms: human, hybrid (half-man, half-creature), and whatever their other form is: animal, bird, fish, insect, etc.

Others like the alien from John Carpenter's *The Thing* (1982), have mutagenic flesh able to shift into many forms, with or without restriction (for example, a monster might only be able to take on the form of something—or someone—it has eaten or otherwise absorbed). Some even steal the memories of the creatures they consume.

Other examples of creatures with mutagenic flesh are the shapeshifters (who actually shed their skin) from various episodes of *Supernatural* (TV, 2005-present) and the Wamphyri (shapeshifting alien vampires) from Brian Lumley's *Necroscope* and *Vampire World* novels (1986-2009). Still more examples are Mystique from *X-Men* (2000), Sylar from *Heroes* (2006-10), and the Changelings from *Star Trek: Deep Space Nine* (TV, 1993-99).

Without magical assistance, assume mutagenic creatures are limited in how far they can stretch or recombine their flesh. A human-sized creature could not transform into Godzilla—there simply isn't enough of it to go around. A safe rule of thumb is a creature can roughly double or halve its size.

Most natural shapeshifters cannot infect humans with their condition as cursed shapeshifters can; however, in some stories, those bitten by a natural shapeshifter become a cursed shapeshifter. Indeed, that could be how the curse came into the world... Other possible sources for natural and cursed shapeshifters are demonic pacts, black magic, or bargains with totem animals.

Most shifters flow easily between forms, typically requiring only a few seconds to a few minutes to fully transform. Nor are they forced to change on the full moon or any other time. They have perfect control over their ability. That's what makes them dangerous.

Something to consider when creating a natural shapeshifter is what its true form really is. For example, is Irena from *Cat People* (1982) really a panther that turns into a woman, or a woman that turns into a panther? That will have a huge impact on how she thinks, acts, and feels. Whichever form she is in, she will have maximized senses, reflexes, and strength to be the best she can be in her present shape. Does that mean she can hear or smell as good in human form as she can as an animal? Probably not, but her senses will still be far superior to those of a normal human.

You can also play around with ideas to mix and match other monsters with shifters, such as an aquatic race of fish people whose hybrid form is mermaids and mermen. You can do the same thing with centaurs and other mythological beings as well.

SAMPLE NATURAL SHAPESHIFTERS

- *Cat People* (1942 and 1982 remake)
- *The Thing* (1982)
- *Manimal* (TV, 1983)
- *It* (1990 and 2017 remake)
- *Stephen King's Sleepwalkers* (1992)
- *Species* (1995)
- *X-Men* (2000)
- *Underworld* series (2003-16)
- *Supernatural* (TV, 2005-present)
- *Heroes* (TV, 2006-10)
- *Blood and Chocolate* (2007)
- *Twilight* (2008)
- *True Blood* (TV, 2008-2014)
- *When Animals Dream* (2014)
- *Wildling* (2018)

NATURAL SHAPESHIFTER PLOT IDEAS

1. A shifter falls in love with a human, which its kind forbids.
2. A shapeshifting alien takes on human form.
3. Shifters decide to end humanity by replacing our leaders and starting a war.
4. A renegade shifter gets hired to be a Mafia assassin.
5. Werewolves are responsible for a series of "animal" attacks.
6. Shifters run a traveling circus posing as both the human staff *and* the animals.
7. A woman hits a dog and tries to take it to the vet, but it's a shifter who turns into a man in her backseat.

9

SUBHUMANS

CAVEMEN ARE THE BLUEPRINT FOR "SUBHUMANS" that are more ape than man (see also cannibals). They are primitive hunter-gatherers who live in caves and want nothing to do with civilized people. They are extremely territorial and aggressive.

Cavemen tribes use crude tools, such as spears, clubs, and axes. They may worship gods, nature, spirits, or their ancestors, but in any case will have a shaman as spiritual leader. The military leader is the war chief. The chief is the overall leader of the tribe and can overrule the decisions of both his shaman and war chief. Tribal succession is either hereditary or by challenge, though shamans will typically be replaced by their apprentice.

Subhumans are not just part of prehistoric times; they can exist in remote regions of the present as well, or tunnel up to the surface after earthquakes as they do in both *Trog* (1970) and *The Pit* (1981). Newly discovered Neanderthals are turned into a savage army by a criminal mastermind in *Hordes of the Red Butcher*, a novel by Grant Stockbridge.

It's also possible to mix subhumans into futuristic settings. Both *The Time Machine* (1960/2002) and *Yor, the Hunter from the Future* (1983) do this. The Reavers from *Firefly* (TV, 2002) and its movie, *Serenity* (2005), explore the terrifying concept of "cavemen in space."

SAMPLE SUBHUMANS

- *One Million B.C.* (1940)
- *The Neanderthal Man* (1953)
- *Monster on the Campus* (1958)
- *Teenage Caveman* (1958)
- *Eegah* (1962)
- *The Time Machine* (1960 and 2002 remake)
- *One Million Years B.C.* (1966)
- *Planet of the Apes* series (1968-73)
- *Trog* (1970)
- *When Dinosaurs Ruled the Earth* (1970)
- *Creatures the World Forgot* (1971)
- *The Land That Time Forgot* (1974)
- *At the Earth's Core* (1976)
- *The Last Dinosaur* (1977)
- *The People That Time Forgot* (1977)
- *The Pit* (1981)
- *Quest for Fire* (1981)
- *Yor, the Hunter from the Future* (1983)
- *Ice Man* (1984)
- *Clan of the Cave Bear* (1986)
- *The 13th Warrior* (1999)
- *Firefly* (TV, 2002)
- *The Descent* series (2005-09)
- *Serenity* (2005)
- *10,000 B.C.* (2008)
- *Ao: The Last Hunter* (2010)

SUBHUMAN PLOT IDEAS

1. A frozen caveman is unthawed and brought to life.
2. Cave explorers discover a tribe of cavemen.

UNDEAD

FRANKENSTEIN'S MONSTER, GHOULS, LICHES, MUMMIES, REVENANTS, SKELETONS, VAMPIRES, ZOMBIES

THE UNDEAD ARE NOT GHOSTS or other incorporeal energy beings like demons. They were once living humans that retain the use of their physical bodies and can easily interact with the physical world. Their souls may be trapped in their body, or may have been removed. If removed, perhaps they are stored elsewhere, such as in a magical object; otherwise, they may have been stolen or destroyed. Or perhaps in your universe, souls don't exist. Perhaps undeath is just another way of life: a mutation, a virus, or symbiotic relationships between the "undead" organism and a human host body.

The final possibility is possession: any trace of the human the undead once was is gone, replaced by an energy being such as a demon, or some kind of re-animating organism such as a virus. In either case, the possessing entity or organism may have access to the memories stored in the host body's brain. This may cause it to mimic the host's behavior, speech patterns, and personality in various ways. This can be intentional, as in the case of an energy being, or unintentional, in the case of an organism.

Corporeal undead make up the classic vampires, mummies, skeletons, and zombies we're all familiar with. What seems to hold true regardless of the type of undead is that they need humans to survive:

either as food, or for a priest or wizard to command them. The primary exception is Frankenstein's monster, which may eat human food, or feed on nothing, or on whatever substance brought it to life instead.

Intelligent undead will be driven to interact with the humans only as sources of amusement, food, or obsession (typically love or revenge). They may hate the living and lash out at them as a way to mourn their own lost humanity, or as a way to justify their superiority, or give meaning to their existence. However, they usually keep their interactions with the living to a minimum, both as a form of self-preservation and to limit any sense of loss from watching loved ones age and die while they go on forever.

Intelligent undead make wonderful villains; being immortal means their goals can be far-reaching and incredibly ambitious. Most take the long view. Since they do not fear death (only their own destruction), they will rarely endanger themselves recklessly, choosing to strategically retreat at the slightest hint of defeat. If pursued by powerful, aggressive, and competent foes, the monster will simply go to ground and hide, waiting for his foes to grow old and die.

Unintelligent undead are much less interesting in and of themselves. What makes them work as villains is either the human (or intelligent undead) commanding them, or else they exist as a force of nature that highlights the strengths and weaknesses of the human characters—the ones they are trying to convert into mindless undead like them.

UNDEAD GOALS AND MOTIVATIONS

As former humans, intelligent undead have many of the same needs as the living: food, shelter, security. Where they differ is in the *nature* of that food. The undead may have different needs for the kind and number of companionship they require, as well as desire for a mate (that is, if they still have a sex drive and ability to perform).

Unintelligent undead have no needs or desires other than to feed and/or obey their masters.

FRANKENSTEIN'S MONSTER

"Frankenstein's monster" refers to a specific type of monster, typically one created by a mad scientist seeking to play God by creating artificial life. That "life" is undead: immortal, emotionally volatile, and possessed of incredible strength. The means by which this monster is created varies: special mineral baths, electrical stimulation, drugs, etc. They may or may not need repeated treatments to continue to function; the default assumption is they don't need any.

This type of undead appears like a pale version of however they appeared in life; if they were stitched together from different corpses, or received an autopsy, or required the mad scientist to operate, there will be scars. These scars can be as awful or as minimal as the surgical skill of their creator allows. The monster experiences little to no physical pain except from fire. It lacks emotional regulation, either feeling too little or too much emotion. It is easily overwhelmed and subject to black and white thinking and negative feedback loops that cause it to retreat from or attack the cause of its pain.

Frankenstein's monsters may desperately want to fit in among the living, or seek their destruction instead. It's quite easy for this undead to develop a superiority complex (it doesn't need to eat or sleep, it cannot age and cannot die except by misadventure). As to its soul, it may or may not be present. If it isn't, then perhaps some other type of energy being has taken up residence in the body: a demon or ghost would be most likely.

Destroying these monsters isn't easy. They must be frozen, electrocuted, burned, or torn apart to stop them.

Even more than the original novel, the classic *Frankenstein* (1931) and *Bride of Frankenstein* (1935) films provide the basis for much of what people know and expect from a Frankenstein story.

Beginning with *The Curse of Frankenstein* (1957), many variant monsters were created by Hammer Films for their *Frankenstein* series (1957-1974); these featured a different creature in each film. In both *The Revenge of Frankenstein* (1958) and *Frankenstein: The True Story* (TV, 1973), the newly created monster begins its unlife attractive and stable, but becomes progressively uglier and more unbalanced over time. Could repeated applications of whatever treatment brought the monster to life prevent this process of decay, or is it inevitable?

Sometimes, dead limbs are grafted onto living bodies. Usually, these are the hands of maniacs, as in Oliver Stone's *The Hand* (1981). Refer to the "Psychic Zombies" section later in this chapter.

H.P. Lovecraft's Re-Animator (1985) introduces a serum-based reanimation procedure that can be used to bring individual parts back to life as well as whole creatures. Depending on how soon after death the serum is administered, the result can be a fully functional undead with its mind more or less intact, or a homicidal zombie.

This type of undead can continue to function even when chopped into pieces. The head continues to think, speak, and bite, the hands continue to grab, the body keeps walking. The head directs the parts telepathically. Destroying the brain stops the individual parts from moving or attacking (also see Psychic Zombies.)

NO SCIENCE, NO MONSTER

Sometimes, the monster is only brought to life in the mind of the madman who creates it. In *Pieces* (1982), the chainsaw killer sews together a patchwork "perfect woman" from the body parts of college girls. Likewise, in *May* (2002), a disturbed young woman decides "if you can't find a friend, make one." She then assembles a patchwork friend out of the body parts of her victims.

The resulting monster doesn't need to be a patchwork doll. In *Maniac* (1980), the killer nails the scalps of his victims to mannequins, which later come to life to murder him... if only in his mind.

Don't feel you must take the concept of creating Frankenstein's monster literally. Sometimes, no organic component is required, only the *belief* the monster is alive, as happens with the ventriloquist dummy in *Magic* (1978) and the sex doll in *Love Object* (2003). Any kind of inanimate object could be breathed to deranged "life" this way, like the preserved corpse of Norman Bates' mother in *Psycho* (1960).

SAMPLE FRANKENSTEIN'S MONSTERS

- *Frankenstein* (1931)
- *Bride of Frankenstein* (1935)
- *Son of Frankenstein* (1939)
- *Ghost of Frankenstein* (1942)
- *Frankenstein Meets the Wolfman* (1943)
- *House of Frankenstein* (1944)
- *House of Dracula* (1945)
- *Abbott and Costello Meet Frankenstein* (1948)
- *Curse of Frankenstein* (1957)
- *I Was a Teenage Frankenstein* (1957)
- *Revenge of Frankenstein* (1958)
- *Evil of Frankenstein* (1960)
- *Frankenstein Conquers the World* (1965)
- *War of the Gargantuas* (1966)
- *Frankenstein Created Woman* (1967)
- *Frankenstein Must Be Destroyed* (1969)
- *Horror of Frankenstein* (1970)
- *Flesh for Frankenstein* (1973)
- *Frankenstein: The True Story* (1973)
- *Frankenstein and the Monster from Hell* (1974)
- *Young Frankenstein* (1974)
- *The Rocky Horror Picture Show* (1975)
- *Terror of Frankenstein* (1977)
- *Magic* (1978)
- *Pieces* (1982)
- *The Bride* (1985)
- *Re-Animator* (1985)
- *Bride of Re-Animator* (1989)
- *Frankenhooker* (1990)
- *Mary Shelley's Frankenstein* (1994)
- *May* (2002)
- *Beyond Re-Animator* (2003)

- *Love Object* (2003)
- *Frankenstein* (2011)
- *Frankenstein's Army* (2013)
- *The Frankenstein Theory* (2013)
- *Hemlock Grove* (TV, 2013-15)
- *Penny Dreadful* (TV, 2014-16)
- *I, Frankenstein* (2014)
- *Frankenstein* (2015)
- *Victor Frankenstein* (2015)
- *The Frankenstein Chronicles* (TV, 2015-17)

FRANKENSTEIN'S MONSTER PLOT IDEAS

1. A mad scientist is stealing body parts to create the "perfect" human.
2. A mad scientist devises an experiment to bring his dead friend/family/lover back to life.
3. The military reanimates dead soldiers as unstoppable "Franken-troopers."

GHOULS

Depending on who you ask, ghouls are shape-shifting demons in physical form, a subhuman race of cunning savages who worship mad gods, or the poor man's cross between a vampire and zombie. What they all have in common is they eat human flesh. Some say they eat only the dead, others say they eat both, but prefer dead victims (who can't fight back).

ARABIC GHOUL

The original ghoul comes from Arabic mythology, where it haunts ruins and wastelands—all the desperate, lonely places of the earth. They can appear as predatory animals (the hyena is a favorite form), or as humans; whatever shape it needs to inspire fear or trust in its victims. The Arabic ghoul is not undead, but a type of djinn (genie), the lowest kind, but that does not mean they are not clever or powerful.

As natural energy beings, they have the power to possess animals or humans; they then use that host body to devour others, and this is where its most devastating power comes in: A ghoul has the ability to take on the appearance of any creature it devours, living or dead. However, upon death, the ghoul's body will revert to whatever shape it first took upon entering the physical world.

This type of ghoul is immortal. Although its physical body can be destroyed, its energy body will return. Note that being killed by this type of ghoul does not cause the victim to become undead.

For my own personal take on Arabic ghouls mixed with viral vampires and zombies, read "The Gift of Flesh" in my short story collection, *Gore Girls*.

SUBHUMAN GHOULS

The second type of ghoul is that popularized by H.P. Lovecraft's Cthulhu Mythos; a race of subhuman savages with sharp teeth who live in underground cities beneath human burial grounds. They tunnel up through the graves to steal the dead bodies for food and to look for human sacrifices for their inhuman gods. Disguised entrances to their tunnels are found in crypts and mausoleums.

These ghouls can take on a more or less normal human appearance, but appear pale and hairless, with rough, rubbery skin and abnormally long, sharp nails. Their true form is similar, but more bestial, with a feral expression and the light of madness burning in their strange, dark eyes. They may be either fat or emaciated, depending on how well they've fed. These ghouls are surprisingly nimble, quick, and possessed of a wiry, inhuman strength.

Since they are not undead, they can be killed in any way a human can—however, their unnatural bodies can take a lot more punishment before expiring. Their rough skin provides reasonable armor in a fight, and its rubbery texture may even stop regular bullets and all but the sharpest objects from doing more than blunt impact damage.

As subterranean creatures, ghouls dislike sunlight and avoid it whenever possible. It does not kill them, but can blind and disorient or give them severe sunburn. As such, they are rarely encountered during daylight hours.

This type of ghoul is not truly undead, but merely a long-lived race, a mutation able to survive hundreds of years. Being killed by this type of ghoul does not cause the victim to become undead, but it is possible for a human to become this type of ghoul: either by choice (undergoing an occult ritual), or by blood; if a ghoul mates with a human, the offspring may appear more or less normal until some point after reaching the point of maturity. At which point, it begins to take on a more ghoul-like appearance. A kind of "psychic homing beacon" will activate in its head, guiding the new ghoul through dreams and visions to the nearest underground community of its kind. The new ghoul's sanity never survives intact.

For the best examples of this type of ghoul, read H.P. Lovecraft's "Pickman's Model," Robert Bloch's "The Grinning Ghoul," and Clive Barker's "The Midnight Meat Train." Also check out *Tokyo Ghoul* (Anime, 2014-2015, and live-action film, 2017).

CURSED GHOULS

The first two types of ghouls are intelligent, driven by alien logic, and capable of organized, methodical plans. This last type is drawn from comic books. It is a cunning but not particularly intelligent type of undead created from the body of a cannibal. It is cursed for this sin to continue to feed on the dead (or the living) until it is destroyed.

This type of ghoul is pale and emaciated, with sharp teeth and strong nails, but it otherwise resembles how it looked when it was alive. It lives in, or lurks near, cemeteries or battlefields, digging out a tunnel network to steal bodies. It cannot eat the living, but has no qualms killing them to eat later, letting them "ripen" (rot) before turning them into a grisly feast.

Those killed by cursed ghouls do not become ghouls themselves unless they willingly ate human flesh or were deceived into becoming cannibals (this type of ghoul enjoys tricking people into suffering its curse, though some may do it in the hope of gaining companionship).

SAMPLE GHOULS

- *The Ghoul* (1933)
- *The Mad Ghoul* (1943)
- *Night Gallery* (TV, 1971, Season 2, Episode 1: "Pickman's Model")
- *The Ghoul* (1975)
- *Castle Freak* (1995)
- *Ghouls* (2008)
- *Midnight Meat Train* (2008)
- *Tokyo Ghoul* (Anime, 2014-2015 and live-action film, 2017)

GHOUL PLOT IDEAS

1. When the cemetery is moved, angry ghouls seek alternative food by hunting humans.
2. The new caretaker at a cemetery begins to suspect ghouls are stealing the bodies.
3. Desert Storm soldiers lost in Iraq are stalked by an Arabic ghoul.

LICHES

A lich is a powerful type of undead driven by ambition and lust for forbidden knowledge. Becoming a lich is a magical process, so most are powerful psychics, priests, or wizards. Those few who are not themselves trained in the required black magic must have paid one who is in order to be transformed (a demonic pact would also work).

The process involves a necromantic ritual that removes both the organs and the soul, placing the soul in a "soul object," such as a gem, amulet, weapon, or phylactery. So long as the soul object remains intact, the lich cannot die. Even if its body is destroyed, its soul can reach out from the object to possess another body (which must typically be a blood relative or someone foolish enough to agree to let the lich possess it).

The lich attempts to dominate its victim, and if it wins, it casts out the former occupant's soul and consumes it. In this case, the host body immediately becomes undead. It begins to take on a progressively more lich-like appearance over the course of several months, though this process can be extended if the body is kept cold and out of sunlight.

So what does a lich look like? It appears as a desiccated corpse with tough, leathery skin stretched tight over its bones like armor. Its eyes are lidless black pits that burn with a sinister, hungry light. At first glance, a lich might be confused for a zombie or ghoul, but it is typically richly dressed or armored, carrying itself proudly. It projects a radius of cold around itself, similar to a ghost.

A lich does not smell of decay. Rather, its scent is dusty, exotic, a bit like a spice rack and similar to mummies in this regard. This is how a lich usually appears for the first several hundred years of its unlife; after that, the skin begins to crack, exposing gaps, and eventually falling away in crepe-like tatters until only bones remain. Like animated skeletons, magic holds the bones together—magic, and sheer force of will.

Liches speak in rasping tones and hissing whispers when they must, but prefer to communicate via telepathy. Whether spoken out loud or through the mind, their default voices are mocking and cruel, their manners condescending and arrogant. They rarely see any need to modify this behavior, caring nothing for how others perceive them.

Liches avoid sunlight as it has a degenerative effect on their skin. However, this process is slow, and a few hours (or even days) of exposure may not produce much effect.

Unlike most other forms of corporeal undead, liches do not feed on flesh or blood; instead they consume psychic energy or "life force" in much the same way as ghosts (see that chapter for details on this process); however, because they are in physical form, they require more energy more often. This causes the victim to age prematurely, wither, and shrivel into a dried-up husk. A victim killed in this manner is simply dead; they do not rise as liches.

Liches make powerful allies, but their ambition, greed, and arrogance means they can rarely be trusted for long. They are driven by cold, twisted logic and see everyone else (living or undead) as inferiors to be tolerated only so long as they prove useful. Combined with their life-draining touch, genius-level I.Q., immortality, and magic abilities, a lich is one of the worst enemies you can make.

For literary examples of liches, read H.P. Lovecraft's "The Thing on the Doorstep," Gardner Fox's "The Sword of the Sorcerer," and Robert E. Howard's *Skull-Face* as well as his short stories, "The Cat and the Skull" and "Scarlet Tears."

Liches are popular in games like *Dungeons & Dragons*, *Warhammer*, and *World of Warcraft*, but there are not many depicted in films. The most famous lich is Lord Voldemort from the *Harry Potter* franchise. Like most liches, Voldemort's only fear is his own death.

For a bizarre psychic alien variation of the lich that also encompasses viral aspects of both vampires *and* zombies (as well as H.P. Lovecraft's Cthulhu Mythos), watch the sci-fi horror movie, *Lifeforce* (1986) or read Colin Wilson's novel, *The Space Vampires*, on which it is loosely based.

SAMPLE LICHES

- *One Dark Night* (1983)
- *Anastasia* (1997)
- *Harry Potter* series (2001-11)
- *Dungeons & Dragons: Wrath of the Dragon God* (2005)
- *Ready Player One* (1018)

LICH PLOT IDEAS

1. A lich hires the hero to recover a rare magical object.
2. A lich wants to possess the body of a blood relative.
3. An elderly wizard sends your hero on a quest to get the things he needs to become a lich.

MUMMIES

Most mummies were created by Egyptian priests thousands of years ago. The mummy's body had all of its organs removed and placed in separate jars (including its brain, which was scooped out by a long hook through its nose so as not to damage the skull). Its skin was treated with various preservatives of oils, herbs, and spices, then it was wrapped in gauze. Due to the dry desert heat and removal of anything that would rot, as well as the protecting bandages, the body desiccates but otherwise remains intact.

Mummies are brought to life by magic. They appear dead until some action is taken that triggers them to reanimate. These conditions will have been set by the priest or wizard who created them, but the most typical one is guarding a pyramid's tomb from thieves and trespassers. When not pursuing its goal, a mummy returns to its dormant state.

Mummies do not need to eat, sleep, or breathe. They move with a slow, shuffling gait. They cannot run. They may have one arm still bound to their chest, with the other outstretched to grab their victims. The chemicals and bandages used to preserve them also function as a kind of leather armor. Lacking internal organs, mummies are immune to piercing damage and ignore most slashing damage. Like skeletons, they fare the worst against blunt force injury, though the bandages keep them from falling apart. They are also particularly susceptible to fire.

VARIANT MUMMIES

The most common variant mummy is that seen in *The Mummy* (1932) and its 1999 remake, in which the mummy retains its intelligence and ambitions. This type of mummy is a trained priest or wizard capable of using magic not only to return to life, but to restore his human appearance even though he remains undead. He may or may not have other mummies or magic at his command. This mummy is free-willed and dangerous, able to blend into human society and use magic to enact whatever his schemes are. He may be seeking a magical object, a reincarnated lost love, to preside over a cult to his gods, or to restore Egypt to greatness.

Two more types of variant mummy are found in the horror film, *Dawn of the Mummy* (1981). The first is the "master mummy," who retains his evil intelligence, and is able to telepathically command an army of "mummy slaves." These mummies act like viral zombies and eat their victims. They also carry "mummy rot," a disease (or magical curse) similar to the zombie virus. Those bitten or or touched by the mummy slaves become infected (cursed). Patches of rot immediately break out in the affected areas, spreading quickly until it reaches the brain and other organs, shutting them down and killing the victim.

The victim rises as a new slave to the master mummy (only without the protective bandages and subject to rot since its organs have not been removed). New slaves must have their brains destroyed to break the telepathic link or be burned to ashes to be killed. Mummified slaves, as well as the master mummy, are made of stronger magic; they must be blown up or burned to ashes.

SAMPLE MUMMIES

- *The Mummy* (1932)
- *The Mummy's Hand* (1940)
- *The Mummy's Tomb* (1942)
- *The Mummy's Curse* (1944)

- *The Mummy's Ghost* (1944)
- *The Aztec Mummy* (1957)
- *The Mummy* (1959)
- *Curse of the Mummy's Tomb* (1964)
- *The Mummy's Shroud* (1967)
- *Blood from the Mummy's Tomb* (1971)
- *The Mummy's Revenge* (1975)
- *The Awakening* (1980)
- *Dawn of the Mummy* (1981)
- *Time Walker* (1982)
- *Tales from the Dark Side: The Movie* (1990)
- *The Mummy* (1999)
- *The Mummy Returns* (2001)
- *Bubba Ho-Tep* (2002)
- *Legion of the Dead* (2005)
- *The Mummy: Tomb of the Dragon Emperor* (2008)
- *The Pyramid* (2014)
- *The Mummy* (2017)

MUMMY PLOT IDEAS

1. Archaeologists begin to die after opening a mummy's tomb.
2. An archaeologist brings a mummy to life and uses it for his own evil ambitions.

REVENANTS

Revenants are corpses brought back to life by the psychic will of a person's soul, or perhaps by making a demonic pact. However they are made, revenants only rise to avenge some terrible injustice or complete some unfinished goal. The nature of that goal can be noble, selfish, or entirely evil...

In *Friday the 13th Part 6* (1986), the goal of undead serial killer Jason Voorhees is to continue to murder promiscuous teenagers and those who enable them... forever. In *Uncle Sam* (1996), the revenant's goal is to murder anyone who isn't "patriotic."

The goal of the revenants in *Deathdream* and *Tales from the Crypt* (both 1972) are simply to get home to their families. They don't even realize they are dead. However, once they do, the question then becomes what next? Do they return to their graves? Do they create a new goal and attempt to carry on? We never find out what happens to the poor fellow in *Tales from the Crypt*, but the revenant in Death-dream becomes increasingly evil, erratic and insane.

Revenants look as they did at the moment they died but may eventually decay until they resemble zombies. If the rot continues, then they must complete their goal before they fall apart. If there is no time limit, then their skin may slowly "toughen up," shrinking into form-fitting leathery armor that makes them even harder to destroy.

And that's the thing—*revenants are tough!* They are strong, motivated, implacable enemies. Nothing stops them: not a bullet to the brain, not a stake through the heart. Only by completely destroying the entire creature can you stop it.

To make matters worse, revenants retain the personality, skills, and memories from when they were alive. They may speak, be telepathic, or unable to make a sound. This ability varies from revenant to revenant; a revenant that was psychic in life (or a wizard) will retain those powers in undeath.

Wounds inflicted on revenants do not heal, though a case could be made for stitching a severed limb back on in such a way that it could function again.

Revenants are uninterested in anyone or anything that does not relate to their goals. So long as you are not on their hit list and do not interfere with them, revenants could care less about you. They do not kill indiscriminately unless they normally did so in life. Revenants are not infectious like viral zombies; those killed by revenants stay dead.

Most of the vengeance-fueled zombies depicted in classic 1950s comic books like *Tales from the Crypt* are revenants, and they were the most common form of non-Voodoo zombie before the flesh-eating variety burst onto the scene in *Night of the Living Dead* (1968).

SAMPLE REVENANTS

- *Children Shouldn't Play with Dead Things* (1972)
- *Deathdream* (1972)
- *Tales from the Crypt* (1972)
- *High Plains Drifter* (1973)
- *Creepshow* (1982)
- *Friday the 13th* series from *Part 6* forward (1986-2003)
- *Creepshow 2* (1987)
- *Maniac Cop* series (1990-93)
- *Sometimes They Come Back* (1991)
- *The Crow* (1994)
- *Uncle Sam* (1996)
- *The Returned* (2004, aka *They Came Back*)
- *The Returned* (2013 and TV, 2015)

REVENANT PLOT IDEAS

1. A dying cop vows justice on the criminals that killed him.
2. A serial killer returns to claim the victims who got away.

SKELETONS

Unlike other types of undead which can be created by curses or science, skeletons require magic (necromancy) to bind their bones together. The god, priest, or wizard who creates them issues a set of orders which the skeletons must obey until destroyed. These orders need to be simple and short, such as "Kill anyone who enters this room, but do not pursue them out of the castle."

Skeletons have no mind or emotions; they cannot be reasoned with, and do not recognize anyone they knew in life. They are set as guards. The number of skeletons a priest or wizard can have in existence at any one time should be limited in some way. Each skeleton could require a separate ritual and sacrifice, perhaps having to be bathed in human blood and rare minerals for a certain time before being ready for reanimation. The choice is yours.

Beyond the idea of magic animating the skeletons, consider if what is really animating the skeletons are ghosts or demons. Also, consider how long the magic lasts.

As seen in *Jason and the Argonauts* (1963) and *Army of Darkness* (1992), skeletons may employ simple weapons and armor to aid them in their assigned tasks. Anything (or anyone) that does not trigger their master's commands is ignored. They do not eat, sleep, or breathe. They ignore piercing and most slashing damage, but are particularly vulnerable to blunt force injury. The magic that reanimates the skeleton is centered in the skull, so destroying the skull destroys the skeleton.

When their orders are triggered, skeletons may show an evil red glow in their eye sockets, or another color if you prefer, or nothing at all. Their bones may be engraved or painted with magic symbols. Skeletons do not speak. Their bones rattle and clack as they move.

VARIANT SKELETONS

The bones of different creatures can be combined in creative ways to create larger, more powerful skeletons. This is particularly effective in fantasy worlds where giant animal and monster bones can be used.

To create an *intelligent skeleton* with (or without) free will, the magic ritual is altered to call back the soul of who the skeleton was in life. Now the skeleton will possess all the skills and knowledge it had before. It will not be able to speak, but can write or, if you wish, communicate telepathically.

Few would choose to come back to life in this manner, so most intelligent skeletons will have been forced into this state and desire to return to death as soon as whatever task they were brought back to life for has been accomplished. Skeleton warriors are the most commonly encountered type of intelligent skeleton. Skeleton pirates can be seen in *Pirates of the Caribbean: The Curse of the Black Pearl* (2003).

Another type of variant skeleton are disembodied skulls invested with psychic or supernatural powers. Such skulls can be seen in *The Screaming Skull* (1958) and *Screaming Skull* (TV, 1973).

In the 1973 horror film, *The Creeping Flesh*, the ancient skeleton of an evil giant regrows flesh when exposed to water. A scientist creates a serum from it that he hopes will inoculate people against evil. He foolishly tests it on his daughter, who promptly goes insane and becomes a murderess.

In *The Skull*, a novel by Shaun Hutson, the unearthed skull of a demonic creature is unearthed in the modern day. Once brought back to the lab for study, a man cuts his hand on it and his blood causes the skull to regrow its flesh (and eventually a body). The newly reformed creature goes on a bloody rampage.

Some heroes and villains have gruesome skull or skull-like faces but human bodies. They are still alive, so they are not true skeletons but still worth noting. The four most famous are Ghost Rider and the Red Skull from Marvel Comics, Dr. Anton Phibes from the *Dr. Phibes* films (1971-72), and Skeletor from *He-Man and the Masters of the Universe* (TV, 1983-85, and the 1987 live-action movie).

SAMPLE SKELETONS

- *Jason and the Argonauts* (1963)
- *The Abominable Dr. Phibes* (1971)
- *Dr. Phibes Rises Again* (1972)
- *The Creeping Flesh* (1973)
- *He-Man and the Masters of the Universe* (TV, 1983-85)
- *Masters of the Universe* (1987)
- *Army of Darkness* (1992)
- *The Nightmare Before Christmas* (1993)
- *Pirates of the Caribbean: The Curse of the Black Pearl* (2003)
- *Ghost Rider* (2007)

- *Captain America: The First Avenger* (2011)
- *Ghost Rider: Spirit of Vengeance* (2011)

SKELETON PLOT IDEAS

1. A necromancer raises skeleton troops to patrol his domain.
2. A cursed skull placed on a headless body reanimates it.

VAMPIRES

Most vampires appear much as they did in life, but are gaunt, pale, with abnormally long and sharp canine teeth and nails. In some variations, the canines and nails may lengthen on command, such as when feeding or in combat. Their irises are dark, almost black, but the pupils may glow when excited, angry, or attempting to hypnotize a victim. Glow color can vary, from fiery red to blazing gold or icy silver. Their skin is cool to the touch. Vampires retain their human intelligence, ambitions, and desires.

It's been over a century since Bram Stoker wrote *Dracula* and ushered in the modern vampire myth. Since then, there have been an infinite number of variations, from *Buffy the Vampire Slayer* (1992) to *Twilight* (2008). That makes presenting a "one size fits all" vampire more difficult—so I'm not even going to try. Instead, I'm going to let you pick and choose your vampire's strengths and weaknesses from the following lists (or invent your own):

VAMPIRE STRENGTHS

- Can Create New Vampires (as slaves or free-willed)
- Command Creatures of the Night (bats, rats, wolves)
- Enhanced Physical Perfection (erasing any scars, tattoos, brands, blemishes it had before dying)

- Enhanced Senses (such as seeing in pitch darkness, hear conversations across a crowded room, etc.)
- Flight
- Hypnotic Gaze (implanting hypnotic suggestions)
- Jump or Fall Great Distances (minimal to no injury)
- Levitation
- Resistance to Physical Damage (and can ignore most pain except sunlight or impalement)
- Shape-change into bats, mist, rats, or wolves
- Super-healing
- Super-strength
- Super-speed
- Telepathy (one way, or two-way with those whose blood it has drunk or who have drunk its blood)
- Wall Climbing (like Spider-Man)
- Weather Control (call storms or darken the area)

VAMPIRE WEAKNESSES

- Cannot Cross Running Water (except by bridge, etc.)
- Cannot Enter a Private Residence without Being
- Invited by a Living Owner or Guest
- Cannot Enter Holy Ground
- Casts No Reflection and Cannot Be Photographed
- Casts No Shadow
- Comatose During the Day
- Hurt or Killed by Decapitation
- Hurt or Killed by Dismemberment
- Hurt or Killed by Fire
- Hurt or Killed by Silver
- Hurt or Killed by Wooden Arrow or Stake Through the Heart
- Hurt or Killed by Sunlight

- Must Feed on Blood (can be Animal or Stored Human Blood)
- Must Feed on Blood (only Fresh Blood from a Living Human)
- Must Feed on Psychic Energy (*Lifeforce*)
- Must Feed on Youth (*Captain Kronos, Vampire Hunter*)
- Must Rest in Its Native Soil to Recharge Its Powers
- Repelled by Garlic
- Repelled by Holy Objects
- Repelled by Mirrors
- Unnaturally Ugly (*Nosferatu, Shadow of the Vampire*)

VAMPIRE BONDING WITH VICTIMS

Once a vampire has drunk the blood of a creature but not killed it, that blood creates a psychic bond, a telepathic link, between vampire and victim. This can be used to send short messages to each other that can be heard over vast distances, or to get brief visions of where the other is and what their emotional state is like.

The bond can also be exploited by vampire hunters, using their own hypnotist on the victim as a way to "see" clues as to where the vampire is.

VAMPIRE FEEDING

Most vampires must drink blood to survive. Failure to consume blood results in starvation, then desiccation and coma. A desiccated, comatose vampire can continue in this state theoretically forever, and can be brought back to life by forcing blood into its mouth.

VAMPIRE SALIVA

A vampire's saliva may include a numbing agent, like a vampire bat. This is so as not to disturb a sleeping or hypnotized victim and allow the vampire to drink its fill. Other vampire saliva contains an "aphrodisiac" effect that makes the act of feeding pleasurable. Some contain both a numbing agent *and* an aphrodisiac.

However, should you not desire your vampire's saliva to have special properties, then the similar effects can be achieved through hypnosis. This requires the vampire to spend more pre-feeding time with the victim, implanting suggestions that the victim loves to be bitten, to be fed on, that it brings pleasure, and they will feel no discomfort.

VAMPIRE HYPNOSIS

Vampires are masters of hypnotism, but hypnotism has its limits. The more time they spend putting the victim into a trance state, the deeper they can implant those suggestions, and the harder they will be to remove.

Note that with hypnosis, phrasing is incredibly important! Negative words are dropped by the subconscious, resulting in the opposite effect. So a vampire who wanted a victim to trust her would never suggest, "You are not afraid of me," because the victim's mind would drop the word "not" and end up with, "You are afraid of me."

The *correct* way to get victims to do what you want is to phrase your suggestions in the positive and present tense, as if they were already true. Using the prior example, the vampire would suggest, "You trust me completely."

Hypnosis cannot make someone do something against their will or that is obviously self-destructive. Those kinds of suggestions will always be rejected and may be jarring enough to break the victim out of the trance state. However, a vampire could convince a victim to do something harmful by assuring them that it is either safe or in their best interest. For example, a vampire floating outside a window ten stories above the ground could not suggest to a victim, "Jump!," but could suggest, "Jump to me! I will catch you."

Imagine the power a vampire posing as a hypnotist could have: an endless supply of victims coming to him and paying for the privilege!

If you plan on having your vampire perform a lot of hypnosis, you should study it and see what it can and can't do. You can always tweak the rules a bit if needed, since your vampire is using it as a supernatural power rather than a trained profession with human limits. However, as with writing, it's important to know the rules before you break them.

VAMPIRE SOCIETY

Vampire: The Masquerade, a popular tabletop and live action role-playing game, set forth the idea of a vampire "shadow society" co-existing in secret with contemporary human society. These vampires were organized into rival noble houses, each composed of a different breed with the same strengths and weaknesses. Each house appointed a member to sit on the ruling Vampire Council to enact laws and policy for all the houses to follow.

This concept of warring noble houses was later borrowed for the Marvel Comics film, *Blade* (1998), and further refined in the superior sequel, *Blade II* (2002). Are the vampires in your story world organized? If so, how?

VAMPIRE BLOOD

In *The Vampire Diaries* (2009-17), vampire blood has healing properties and can be used to save the life of humans. However, if the human dies with vampire blood still in its system, the human becomes a vampire. It takes a day for the blood to be eliminated from the system.

True Blood (2008-2014) takes this a step further by also making it an addictive drug that enhances the senses and libido, as well as strength. It causes hallucinations and erotic dreams.

House of Dracula (1945) takes a different tactic. In that film, vampire blood transfusions turn humans evil in thought *and* appearance. One way to develop that concept further would be turning the humans into "were-vampires"—normal by day, bloodsuckers by night!

What properties does vampire blood have in your world?

BECOMING A VAMPIRE

There are typically three ways to become a vampire, but you can decide which are true and which are false or invent your own:

1. Exsanguination (death by vampiric blood drain);
2. Dying with the blood of a vampire in your system; or
3. Magic: either a demonic pact or cursed by a god.

If the new vampire was not created by magic, you need to decide if it is telepathically linked, psychically bonded, or enslaved to the vampire who killed it or whose blood it drank. Whatever they are, the new vampires will be thirsty!

VARIANT: SCIENCE-BASED VAMPIRES

Tired of undead vampires? What about a virus or biological warfare creating mutant living vampires? Read Richard Matheson's classic sci-fi horror novel, *I Am Legend* (1954), which was adapted three times into film as *The Last Man on Earth* (1964), *The Omega Man* (1971), and *I Am Legend* (2007). Another mutant vampire movie to watch is David Cronenberg's *Rabid* (1977), which mixes elements of vampires and zombies with the disturbing "body horror" subgenre Cronenberg is known for.

SAMPLE VAMPIRES

- *Nosferatu* (1922 and 1979 remake)
- *Dracula* (1931 and 1979 remake)
- *Dracula's Daughter* (1936)
- *Son of Dracula* (1943)
- *The Return of the Vampire* (1943)
- *House of Frankenstein* (1944)
- *House of Dracula* (1945)

- *Abbott and Costello Meet Frankenstein* (1948)
- *Horror of Dracula* (1958)
- *The Return of Dracula* (1958)
- *The Brides of Dracula* (1960)
- *Black Sabbath* (1963)
- *The Last Man on Earth* (1964)
- *Dr. Terror's House of Horrors* (1965)
- *Dracula: Prince of Darkness* (1966)
- *Dark Shadows* (TV, 1966-71)
- *The Fearless Vampire Killers* (1967)
- *Dracula Has Risen from the Grave* (1968)
- *Count Yorga, Vampire* (1970)
- *Scars of Dracula* (1970)
- *Taste the Blood of Dracula* (1970)
- *The Vampire Lovers* (1970)
- *Lust for a Vampire* (1971)
- *The Omega Man* (1971)
- *The Return of Count Yorga* (1971)
- *Twins of Evil* (1971)
- *Blacula* (1972)
- *Deathmaster* (1972)
- *Dracula A.D. 1972* (1972)
- *Night of the Devils* (1972)
- *The Night Stalker* (TV, 1972)
- *Bram Stoker's Dracula* (TV, 1973)
- *Count Dracula's Great Love* (1973)
- *Crypt of the Living Dead* (1973)
- *The Devil's Wedding Night* (1973)
- *The Satanic Rites of Dracula* (1973)
- *Scream, Blacula, Scream* (1973)
- *The Vampires Night Orgy* (1973)
- *Vault of Horror* (1965)
- *Blood for Dracula* (1974)
- *Captain Kronos, Vampire Hunter* (1974)
- *Legend of the Seven Golden Vampires* (1974)

- *Vampyres* (1974)
- *Count Dracula* (1977)
- *Dracula's Dog* (1978, aka *Zoltan, Hound of Dracula*)
- *Martin* (1978)
- *Dracula* (1979)
- *'Salem's Lot* (TV, 1979)
- *Thirst* (1979)
- *The Hunger* (1983)
- *Fright Night* (1985)
- *The Lost Boys* (1987)
- *The Monster Squad* (1987)
- *Near Dark* (1987)
- *Bram Stoker's Dracula* (1992)
- *Buffy the Vampire Slayer* (1992)
- *Innocent Blood* (1992)
- *Interview with the Vampire* (1994)
- *From Dusk till Dawn* (1996)
- *Buffy the Vampire Slayer* (TV, 1996-2003)
- *The Night Flier* (1997)
- *Blade* (1998)
- *Vampires* (1998)
- *Shadow of the Vampire* (2000)
- *Blade 2* (2002)
- *30 Days of Night* (2007)
- *Let the Right One In* (2008 and 2010 remake, *Let Me In*)
- *The Vampire Diaries* (TV, 2009-17)
- *Stake Land* (2010)
- *Being Human* (TV, 2011-2014)
- *Hemlock Grove* (TV, 2013-15)
- *Dracula Untold* (2014)
- *What We Do in the Shadows* (2014)
- *Penny Dreadful* (TV, 2014-16)
- *The Strain* (TV, 2014-2017)
- *Living Among Us* (2018)

VAMPIRE PLOT IDEAS

1. A construction crew digs up a corpse with a stake through its heart.
2. A vampire with amnesia wakes up in a coffin thinking she's been buried alive.
3. A suspected serial killer turns out to be a vampire.

ZOMBIES

Zombies are mindless monsters created from dead bodies. They come in five types, including those brought back by:

1. Demons
2. Psychic energy
3. Science
4. Viruses
5. Voodoo (or other magic)

Most are slaves ("hosts") to whatever force reanimated them.

DEMONIC ZOMBIES

Demonic zombies are reanimated corpses that blend cunning, cruelty, and super-strength. Some can teleport or transform their bodies into terrifying shapes. They may appear alive until they attack.

These zombies may or may not eat human flesh; their primary purpose is to torment, infect, and murder the living, with bonus points for damning the souls of their victims while creating another host body to possess. Those killed by them may or may not reanimate. Whether or not they do depends on the rules you create:

1. Is it a psychic or spiritual virus that requires victim consent to kill its host as in a traditional demonic possession movie?

Then not every corpse reanimates, only those too weak to resist the demon's evil.

2. Is it a physical virus with a psychic or supernatural component that does *not* require victim consent? Then it will automatically kill its host, as in a traditional virus zombie movie.

The "Deadites" from Sam Raimi's *Evil Dead* films are a prime example of the first option, while the *[REC]* and *Quarantine* series zombies are examples of the second.

Note that with demonic zombies, sometimes most of the zombies aren't very smart and act like regular virus zombies, while the ringleader zombie (often in the body of a defrocked priest or warlock) has telepathic command over them. Both Lucio Fulci's *City of the Living Dead* (1980) and *The Beyond* (1981) deal with demonic ringleader zombies opening the "gates of hell" that allow the demonic dead to rise.

In *Messiah of Evil* (1973), demonic zombies are created by a spiritual virus, curse, or other unseen supernatural force. In Stephen King's *Pet Sematary* (1989), they are created by burying the dead in a cursed native burial ground; evil spirits (possibly related to the Wendigo) bring them back to life.

The last type of demonic zombie are the dried-out reanimated corpses of the devil-worshipping Knights Templar seen in *Tombs of the Blind Dead* (1972) and its three sequels. These undead knights are clad in robes and armor, wield swords, and rise from their graves to drink the blood of the living. Though they cannot speak, they can still think, and coordinate their attacks both on foot and horseback, riding skeletal war horses. They cannot see, hence their name ("The Blind Dead"), but rather rely on their keen sense of hearing to track victims.

The Blind Dead mix certain qualities of liches, mummies, revenants, skeletons, and vampires, so they are a bit hard to classify. I've included them here because they owe their unlife to a pact with the Devil.

SAMPLE DEMONIC ZOMBIES

- *Tombs of the Blind Dead* (1972)
- *Messiah of Evil* (1973)
- *Return of the Blind Dead* (1973)
- *The Ghost Galleon* (1974, aka *Horror of the Zombies*)
- *Night of the Seagulls* (1975, aka *Night of the Death Cult*)
- *The Beyond* (1981)
- *The Evil Dead* (1981 and 2013 remake)
- *City of the Living Dead* (1983, aka *The Gates of Hell*)
- *Demons* (1985)
- *Demons 2* (1986)
- *Evil Dead 2* (1987)
- *Flesheater* (1988)
- *Night of the Demons* (1988 and 2009 remake)
- *Pet Sematary* (1989)
- *Army of Darkness* (1992)
- *Pet Sematary 2* (1992)
- *Night of the Demons 2* (1994)
- *Tales from the Crypt: Demon Knight* (1995)
- *Night of the Demons 3* (1997)
- *[REC]* (2007)
- *Quarantine* (2008)
- *[REC] 2* (2009)
- *Quarantine 2* (2011)
- *JeruZalem* (2015)
- *Ash vs. Evil Dead* (TV, 2015-2018)

PSYCHIC ZOMBIES

Psychic zombies are powered by a combination of telepathy and psychokinesis (aka telekinesis). A living psychic, a ghost, a demon, or some other energy being brings a corpse or severed body part back to "life" and uses it to gain revenge or complete some other objective.

These parts can remain unattached or may have been transplanted onto another human. They often belonged to "mad stranglers" in life.

Variants may be powered by science or radiation, but regardless of origin, no psychic zombie is truly undead.

Films featuring psychic zombies are:

- *Mad Love* (1933)
- *The Beast with Five Fingers* (1946)
- *Hands of a Stranger* (1962)
- *Dr. Terror's House of Horrors* (1965)
- *And Now the Screaming Starts* (1973)
- *The Severed Arm* (1973)
- *Demonoid* (1981)
- *The Hand* (1981)
- *One Dark Night* (1983)
- *Evil Dead 2* (1987)
- *Body Parts* (1991)
- *Idle Hands* (1999)

SCIENCE ZOMBIES

Science zombies can be the mindless kind or those that retain their intelligence (if not their souls). Some are true undead, others only appear that way. Those killed by science zombies stay dead.

In the science fiction films, *Invisible Invaders* and *Plan 9 from Outer Space* (both 1959), aliens use the bodies of the dead to attack humanity. The aliens in *Invisible Invaders* are energy beings that physically merge with corpses, wearing them like "meat suits" in order to interact with the physical world. *Plan 9*'s aliens operate the zombies by remote control "radio waves" from their spaceship. Experimental sonic technology also bring the dead back to life in *The Living Dead at the Manchester Morgue* (1974, aka *Let Sleeping Corpses Lie*).

The 1973 TV movie, *The Night Strangler*, features a Civil War-era mad scientist creating an "elixir of life" from the spinal fluid of beautiful women. The elixir must be injected every 21 years, and has the effect of sustaining the scientist's physical body (as well as giving it super-strength). If he does not receive another dose after 21 years, he begins to age and rot until he crumbles to dust.

Similar to *The Night Strangler*, undead mad scientist Dr. Freudstein sustains his nightmarish existence through alchemy and murder in Lucio Fulci's *House by the Cemetery* (1981). The main difference between these two scientists is The Night Strangler appears human, while Dr. Freudstein is slimy, rotting, and full of maggots.

Depending on when they are revived by mad scientist Herbert West's serum, the zombies in *Re-Animator* (1985) can be anything from violent morons to every bit as smart as they were when alive.

Another example of an intelligent zombie created (at least in part) by science is in David Wellington's novel, *Monster Island*. A medical student in a viral zombie outbreak commits suicide, but takes every possible precaution to preserve his brain function. The experiment works! Although still a flesh-eating zombie, he has retained his personality, emotions, and memories, as well as a high degree of self-control around those tasty humans. He also gains the ability to command other zombies.

SAMPLE SCIENCE ZOMBIES

- *Invisible Invaders* (1959)
- *Plan 9 from Outer Space* (1959)
- *The Night Strangler* (TV, 1973)
- *The Living Dead at the Manchester Morgue* (1974, aka *Let Sleeping Corpses Lie*)
- *Shock Waves* (1977)
- *House by the Cemetery* (1981)

VIRUS ZOMBIES

This zombie is the modern, flesh-eating kind. They are the means by which the zombie virus spreads itself, serving as mobile disease platforms. They infect others through biting, clawing, or transmission of bodily fluids. Once infected, a person develops a high fever, sickening and dying within a few days at most. Those who die as a result are reanimated by the virus. They get up (as best as they can, depending on their injuries), and begin wandering aimlessly until they locate food. That food is uninfected humans.

Zombie vision is poor, so they rely on their sense of hearing and smell to track prey. They never tire, so it's impossible to outrun them. You can lose them (so long as you don't run away in a straight line), or trick them into following something noisier or easier to catch. If you are trapped, zombies will try to break in to eat you. If they fail, they'll wait around for you to come out or until something easier comes along.

Zombies have a blank expression, an empty gaze, and show various signs of injury and decomposition depending on how they died and how long they have been dead. They walk with an awkward, shuffling gait that can sometimes (if they are fresh enough) become a short, clumsy run when food is nearby.

Some may use simple tools like rocks or sticks as bludgeoning weapons, or sharp objects like knives, especially if they died with them still clutched in their hands. A rare few who were trained in firearms may remember how to shoot, but not reload, nor will their aim be accurate. For an example, watch *Day of the Dead* (1985).

Generally, the zombie will retain one or two quirks of its former human self. Some may even attempt to do things they did in life, performing skills like drive a car or actions like go shopping at their favorite store. These may give the zombie character, but they don't give it humanity, or true intelligence. They are "ghost behaviors," left-over patterns and impulses that the zombie virus has not yet over-written. On some level, the virus may even encourage these behaviors if they help it find food.

In the initial stages of a zombie apocalypse, zombies will be fresh, and may not appear to be obviously dead. This, combined with no one knowing what a zombie is yet, makes it easy for the virus to spread.

A reanimated zombie initially appears confused, almost as if they are trapped in a dream, but this confusion quickly vanishes, replaced by hunger and aggression. New zombies may also experience flashes of recognition of the people they knew when they were alive; this can result in the zombie hesitating to attack those people (if they loved them). Presented with a choice between someone they loved and someone they didn't, a "fresh" zombie will almost always choose to attack the person they did not know or love. Of course, various factors may prevent the zombie from selecting that person; these could be distance, difficulty, or the interference of the person they know.

Zombies are driven by hunger. They live to kill and kill to eat, infecting as many as they can along the way. Zombies can only be killed by destroying the brain, which is where the virus is centered. A zombie with its head cut off can still bite, a zombie with its legs blown off can still crawl. They keep coming. And they want to make you just like them. That's what makes them scary.

The zombie virus may be man-made, or a natural or supernatural mutation, even a magical curse, but it's origin isn't important. In fact, it's a terrible idea to explain why the dead are rising; no one has ever gotten it right and only looked stupid for trying. That's not to say you can't have characters in your story *try* to explain it, but only as conjecture. No definitive explanation should be given. Trust me, you can't get clever here.

Whatever reason you have for why flesh-eating zombies exist, keep it to yourself. Your readers don't care, and more than that, *they don't want to know*. I'm telling you this as horror fan who has watched virtually every zombie movie ever made. The ones that try to explain it always suck. Instead, just let the zombie apocalypse happen. That's the fun, that's the fear: *Not knowing why.*

INTELLIGENT ZOMBIES

Intelligent fast zombies can be found in *Return of the Living Dead* (1985); they are created by a military nerve gas. They can talk and reason to a degree, but are in incredible pain, a pain that is only temporarily lessened by eating live human brains (or inflicting pain on themselves, as seen in *Return of the Living Dead 3*). Anyone killed by these zombies or exposed to the gas that created them becomes a zombie.

Another intelligent zombie, if not as fast or smart, is "Bub" from George Romero's *Day of the Dead* (1985). Bub is a standard flesh-eating shambler, but one who has been "domesticated" by a mad scientist and taught to remember pieces of his old human life. As long as he is fed and treated kindly, Bub remains tame and loyal.

A third type of intelligent zombie exists: former zombies "cured" by science (or magic) and restored to life of one kind of another. This concept is explored in the BBC TV series, *In the Flesh* (2013-14), and the films *The Returned* (2004), *Warm Bodies* (2013), and *The Cured* (2017). What rights do formerly dead people have? Can they relapse into their former savage state?

Some newly risen zombies start off intelligent, but as the rot sets in, so does the savagery. Eventually, they become mindless killing machines. This is explored in *My Boyfriend's Back* (1993), *Boy Eats Girl* (2005), and *Life After Beth* (2014).

Infected people losing their minds as they turn into zombies can be seen in *Colin* (2008), *Contracted* (2013) and its sequel, *Contracted: Phase 2* (2015) and in the "New Year's Day" episode of *Fear Itself* (TV, 2008).

FAST VS. SLOW ZOMBIES

Personally, I favor classic, slow-moving zombies. When you try to make zombies "more extreme," you're just making it harder to suspend disbelief. How does a regular human die and come back to life as an undead track star?

The other problem with fast zombies is it ruins the fantasy. Many zombie fans want to at least *pretend* they have a chance to survive in a post-apocalyptic world. As soon as the zombies run faster then they can, their chances of survival go from slim to none. That may be "extreme," but it's not realistic.

One way around the believability issue of fast zombies is to substitute living maniacs created by a virus instead (see the chapter on Human Monsters for more on "Virus Maniacs" like those found in *The Crazies* and *28 Days Later*).

SAMPLE VIRUS ZOMBIES

- *Night of the Living Dead* (1968 and 1990 remake)
- *Dawn of the Dead* (1978 and 2004 remake)
- *Burial Ground: The Nights of Terror* (1981)
- *Hell of the Living Dead* (1981, aka *Night of the Zombies*)
- *Day of the Dead* (1985)
- *Return of the Living Dead* (1985)
- *Night of the Creeps* (1986)
- *Dead Heat* (1988)
- *Return of the Living Dead 2* (1988)
- *Braindead* (1992, aka *Dead Alive*)
- *My Boyfriend's Back* (1993)
- *Return of the Living Dead 3* (1993)
- *Cemetery Man* (1994, aka *Dellamorte Dellamore*)
- *Bio Zombie* (1998)
- *Resident Evil* series (2002-16)
- *Shaun of the Dead* (2004)
- *Boy Eats Girl* (2005)
- *Land of the Dead* (2005)
- *Severed: Forest of the Dead* (2005)
- *Fido* (2006)
- *Diary of the Dead* (2007)
- *Flight of the Living Dead: Outbreak on a Plane* (2007)
- *Colin* (2008)
- *Dead Set* (TV miniseries, 2008)
- *Deadgirl* (2008)
- *Fear Itself* (TV, 2008, "New Year's Day" episode)
- *Dead Air* (2009)

- *Dead Snow* (2009)
- *The Horde* (2009)
- *Survival of the Dead* (2009)
- *Zombieland* (2009)
- *The Dead* (2010)
- *Highschool of the Dead* (Anime, 2010)
- *Juan of the Dead* (2010)
- *Rammbock* (2010, aka *Berlin Undead*)
- *Contracted* (2013)
- *The Dead 2: India* (2013)
- *The Walking Dead* (TV, 2011-present)
- *The Battery* (2012)
- *Warm Bodies* (2013)
- *World War Z* (2013)
- *Contracted: Phase 2* (2013)
- *In the Flesh* (TV, 2013-14)
- *Life After Beth* (2014)
- *Wyrmwood: Road of the Dead* (2014)
- *Extinction* (2015)
- *Fear the Walking Dead* (TV, 2015-present)
- *Maggie* (2015)
- *The Rezort* (2015)
- *Seoul Station* (Anime, 2016)
- *Train to Busan* (2016)
- *Cargo* (2017)
- *The Night Eats the World* (2018)

VIRUS ZOMBIE PLOT IDEAS

1. Survivors are trapped by a quarantine around their town.
2. Your hero must flee a city infested with hungry zombies.
3. A team of scientists race against time to find a cure.
4. Survivors take to the road after losing their shelter.
5. A cursed tomb is opened, unleashing centuries-old zombies.

VOODOO ZOMBIES

Depending on if magic is real in your story, these can be true undead or else the result of being given a dose of *tetrodotoxin*, a neurotoxin derived from puffer fish venom that causes the victim to appear dead. Before death can occur, however, the victim is given an antidote along with a dose of *datura stramonium*, a plant-based drug with strong hallucinogenic and alleged mind control properties. The victim is then convinced by the Voodoo *bokor* (wizard) that he is now not only dead, but a zombie, and his soul has been stolen by the bokor and will not be returned unless the zombie obeys his commands.

Voodoo zombies are used as slaves in Haiti, frequently on plantations either around the clock or as the "night crew," so as not to upset those who work the fields by day. Zombies are created from those the priest hates or desires to control, or from those who won't be missed so the bokor can profit by turning them into zombies.

Voodoo zombies are incredibly hard to kill; they don't feel pain and will attempt to follow whatever the last order they were given until destroyed. Undead zombies are not immortal and will break down over time until they become useless. However, the bokor will get many years (often decades) of work out of them before this happens. If fed salt, Voodoo zombies must return to their graves peacefully and lay down to die; they cannot be reanimated again after this, as it also frees their souls from the bokor's bondage.

Zombies created by drugs are not undead and can be killed normally (though due to their drug-induced state, they ignore pain and keep coming until suffering crippling injury). They may be incapable of coherent speech or precise motion, and may or may not recognize the people they knew in life. They are emotionally flat, speaking slowly if at all. Their brains are hopelessly broken, their will shattered. They exhibit various symptoms of severe mental illness, such as schizophrenia or catatonia. They may not be able to do much of anything for themselves unless ordered to, and are prone to wandering away if left unsupervised.

SAMPLE VOODOO ZOMBIES

- *White Zombie* (1932)
- *Black Moon* (1936)
- *Ouanga* (1936)
- *Revolt of the Zombies* (1936)
- *King of the Zombies* (1941)
- *I Walked with a Zombie* (1943)
- *Revenge of the Zombies* (1943)
- *Voodoo Man* (1944)
- *Zombies on Broadway* (1945)
- *Voodoo Island* (1957)
- *Voodoo Woman* (1957)
- *Zombies of Mora Tau* (1957)
- *Plague of the Zombies* (1966)
- *I Eat Your Skin* (1971)
- *Isle of the Snake People* (1971)
- *Asylum* (1972)
- *Sugar Hill* (1974)
- *Zombie* (1979, aka *Zombi 2*)
- *Dead and Buried* (1981)
- *The Serpent and the Rainbow* (1988)
- *Voodoo* (1995)
- *Ritual* (2002)

VOODOO ZOMBIE PLOT IDEAS

1. Migrant farm workers are turned into zombie slaves.
2. A man inherits a plantation staffed by zombie slaves.
3. A Voodoo curse creates a spiritual virus that mimics the effects of flesh-eating zombies.
4. A grieving mother goes looking for her missing son in Haiti only to discover he's been turned into a zombie.

AFTERWORD

THERE IS NO LIMIT TO EVIL, just as is there is no limit to your imagination. This book gives you the tools to create any kind of monster you want, from the "classics" to the most modern, even the human kind. But what does it mean to be a monster? What does it mean to live outside the law—not just the laws of man, but the laws of nature or even space and time?

How would that change you?

Most everything man does is based on his fear of dying, of creating a legacy, whether through children or his work. And then there's the whole "you only live once" message—that you better have fun now because you may not get the chance again. There's always something ready to stand in the way of pleasure, from a drunk driver to cancer to the hopeless grind of dull days trying to make ends meet. Before you know it, you're dead, and chances are, you have more than a few regrets to keep you and the worms company.

But what if you were immortal? What if dying was no longer an issue? How would that change your decisions? How would that change your life? What if you could command magic or alien technology to do the impossible? How interested would you be in making the world a "better place"? Wouldn't you want to reshape it into *your* place? A place where you were no longer the monster, the outcast, but in control? And oh, how you'd make those pesky humans dance—if you allowed them to remain at all.

Monsters think differently from us because they are different. From the moment they are born to the moment they die, they struggle in ways we can never understand.

— JACKSON DEAN CHASE
Get a free book at
www.JacksonDeanChase.com

P.S.: If you enjoyed this book, please leave a review to help others in their author journey.

WHAT'S NEXT?

Now that you've mastered the basics of creating monsters and maniacs, it's time to move on to more specific goals:

- *Writing Dynamite Story Hooks* walks you through how to emotionally hook readers step by step, line by line regardless of what genre you write.

- *Writing Heroes & Villains* covers how to create all kinds of heroes and villains, as well as supporting cast, teams, and minor characters. You'll also learn how to quickly master writing men and women in your fiction.

- *Writing Apocalypse & Survival* takes you into the apocalyptic and post-apocalyptic genres, giving you complete, infinitely expandable plot templates as well everything you need to know about what happens when the world ends. The book covers zombies, *Mad Max*-style road warriors, and more.

If you need help describing things—and I do mean anything—than be sure and grab my *Writers' Phrase Books*:

- #1 Horror
- #2 Post-Apocalypse
- #3 Action
- #4 Fantasy
- #5 Fiction (a short series sampler)
- #6 Science Fiction
- #7 Romance, Emotion, and Erotica

Note that the phrase books are intended as standalones, so all but the Romance one repeat a lot of the same action descriptions. You may not need to own more than one or two of these phrase books.

That's all till next time. Thank you for buying my book and I hope to see you again soon.

— JACKSON DEAN CHASE
Get a free book at
www.JacksonDeanChase.com

P.S.: If you enjoyed this book, please leave a review to help others on their author journey.

APPENDIX 1: MONSTER BUILDER

STEP 1: MONSTER BUILDER

There are 97 key questions you need to ask yourself when creating a realistic monster or other non-human race—whether it is unique or one of many.

Non-intelligent or animal-like creatures require less detail, but for human- or higher-level creatures, you should answer all the applicable questions. If you aren't sure how to answer, leave it blank and come back to it later.

1. What is the monster's name?
2. What is the monster's species and subtype?
3. Where does the monster come from?
4. What is the monster's native habitat?
5. How long has it lived there?
6. How long has it been on earth or your story world (if that is not its native habitat)?
7. If non-native to its current habitat, how did it get here?
8. Was its coming here by choice or was it forced to?
9. Does it desire to stay here or return to its native world?

10. How has it adapted its native and/or adopted habitat?
11. Is there anything that restricts it ability to travel outside its native habitat?
12. What is the monster's preferred diet, and how often must it feed?
13. What food makes it thrive above all others?
14. What happens if it consumes too much food?
15. What food makes it weaken, sicken, or die?
16. What happens if it starves to death?
17. How does the monster communicate and what language(s) does it know?
18. How fluent is it in these languages?
19. What does its native language sound like?
20. Does it have any common short expressions or slang in its language? If yes, write them as they sound in English, but keep them as phonetic as possible and limit or avoid the use of special characters.
21. How intelligent and cunning is the monster compared to the average human (I.Q.)?
22. How intelligent and cunning is it compared to the average member of its race or kind?
23. What are the monster's mental strengths?
24. What are its mental weaknesses?
25. How strong is the monster compared to the average human?
26. How strong is it compared to the average member of its race or kind?
27. How do the monster's supernatural and/or psychic powers compare to the average human?
28. How do its supernatural and/or psychic powers compare to the average member of its kind?
29. What are the monster's physical strengths?
30. What are its physical weaknesses?
31. What are the monster's supernatural and/or psychic powers?

32. How do the monster's supernatural and/or psychic powers compare to the average human's?
33. How do its supernatural and/or psychic powers compare to the average member of its race or kind?
34. Who or what does the monster love and desire?
35. Who or what does it hate and despise?
36. Who or what does it fear?
37. What is the monster's primary goal?
38. What is its secondary goal?
39. What is its tertiary goal?
40. What are its other goals?
41. What is it willing to sacrifice its goals for?
42. What is it willing to sacrifice its life for?
43. What is it willing to sacrifice its soul for?
44. Does the monster have a gender and how does it express it?
45. Does it reproduce, and if so, how?
46. Can it mate with humans to produce offspring?
47. Will the human mother die giving birth?
48. What will the monster/human hybrid child be like?
49. What does the monster's true form look like?
50. What color is its skin? What color is its hair?
51. What color are its eyes?
52. What color is its blood?
53. What color are its teeth, claws, and/or horns?
54. What does the monster smell like?
55. Can it take on other forms or appearances? If yes, how does it do this?
56. What does the transformation look like and what noises and/or smells does it produce?
57. How long does it take for it to change its form(s) or appearance(s)?
58. What is the monster's average lifespan?
59. How old is it now?
60. Is this considered a child, teenager, adult, or elder of its kind?

61. 17. How does the monster relate to other creatures?
62. Does it have a concept of family, and if so, what is it?
63. Does it prefer to travel in packs or groups of its own kind?
64. Does it travel with other monsters or anyone else?
65. Does it travel with others by choice or by force?
66. What are the monster's beliefs or opinions on: magic, psychic phenomena, the supernatural, human society?
67. What does it do for fun or a hobby?
68. Does it ever drink, use drugs, or engage in other addictive behaviors?
69. How often is the monster bored and by what?
70. Does it value human currency and valuables?
71. Does its race or kind have or produce its own currency?
72. Is it willing to barter for goods or services, and if yes, what would it typically offer in a barter?
73. Is the monster: amoral, iImmoral, moral, or does it operate by its own twisted moral code?
74. What are its social taboos?
75. What is its view on crime?
76. What is its view on murder?
77. What is its view on sex?
78. What is its view on war?
79. What is its view on art?
80. What is its view on craft and commerce?
81. Can it feel and express empathy or sympathy for others?
82. Is there anything it *won't* do to get what it wants?
83. Is there anything it *wants* to do, but feels conflicted about?
84. Can its "better nature" be appealed to?
85. What government does the monster have?
86. Does it prefer to rule or be ruled by might or merit?
87. Who is it willing to accept as its ruler/master?
88. Who is it *not* willing to accept as its ruler/master?
89. What is the monster's religion?
90. What god (or gods) does it worship?
91. Does it worship out of love or fear?

92. What is its view on the afterlife?
93. What is its view on the Spirit World?
94. What is the monster's preferred shelter?
95. Where *can't* it take shelter?
96. Does the monster use or create its own technology or rely on that of others?
97. What kind of technology does the monster produce?

APPENDIX 2: MAGIC SPELLS

What is magic? It is the art of imposing your will on the universe through the manipulation of natural and supernatural forces. If your monster knows how to cast spells, you need to decide what spells it knows and whether it can cast them innately (which implies it knows a limited number) or whether they must be learned—in which case, the number of spells it knows is limited only by its education and access to magical books and/or mentoring.

To determine what type of spells a monster knows, think of the type of magic it needs in order to perform its story goals. It should not know and be good at all types of magic or it will not only be too powerful, but boring.

LIMITS OF MAGIC

Magic systems are important because when the author knows the rules, he knows what magic can and can't do, which creates consistency and credibility.

One of the worst things you can do as an author is make a magic item or spell that's *too good*. Readers will wonder why the hero (or villain) simply doesn't use it all the time to solve their problems and short-circuit the plot. The usual workaround is to impose limits on how and when the spell can be cast or item used. These limits must make sense, and there must be a very real penalty for violating that limit.

Here are ideas for limitations per use of a spell or item:

- Rare and costly material components or a sacrifice
- Specific rare event must be occurring (eclipse, etc.)
- Must perform a quest, pact, or other action
- Life force drain (fast aging) or worse, *soul drain*
- More than one use causes permanent insanity
- More than one use is impossible (or fatal)

TYPES OF MAGIC

Here are seven types of magic, what they are primarily concerned with achieving, and sample spells from each:

ABJURATION (PROTECTION MAGIC)

- Cloaking Spell (hides its location from senses or magic)
- Dispel Magic (blocks magical attacks or activity in its vicinity)
- Force Field (blocks physical attacks from all directions simultaneously)
- Invisible Shield (blocks physical attacks from only one side at a time)
- Remove Curse (curse is either broken or transferred to another eligible party)
- Ward (may be protection against all damage, one type, or several types, to an area, or individuals)

CONJURATION (SUMMONING MAGIC)

- Banish Summoned Creatures or Objects
- Open Gate to Another Dimension
- Open Gate to Another Part of Same World
- Summon Animals (all types or specific kind)
- Summon/Store Energy (all types or specific kind)
- Summon/Store Magic (all types or specific kind)
- Summon Monsters (all types or specific kind)
- Summon Objects (all types or specific kind)
- Summon People (specific individuals only)
- Psychokinesis (aka Telekinesis)
- Teleportation

ENCHANTMENT (MIND MAGIC)

- Alter Dream
- Alter Emotion
- Alter Perceptions
- Cause Seizure
- Create Confusion
- Create or Remove Mental Illness
- Influence Others
- Mind Control
- Put Self or Others to Sleep (short term)
- Put Self or Others into Magical Hibernation
- Quicken Self (moves fast for a brief duration)
- Telepathy (one-way or two-way)

ILLUSION (DISGUISE AND MISDIRECTION MAGIC)

- Appear as Other

- Blur (harder to see and hit in combat)
- Hallucination (single target sees and/or hears something that isn't real)
- Mass Hallucination (multiple targets see and/or hear something that isn't real)
- Invisibility (monster becomes invisible for a limited duration or under specific conditions)
- Manipulate Light and Shadow (brighten or darken a limited area to blind or mislead, awe, or frighten. Can also create light or shadow-based illusions.)

NATURE (POSITIVE ENERGY MAGIC)

- Alter Temperature Around Self or Others
- Banish Negative Energy
- Banish Unnatural Creatures or Objects
- Breathe Underwater
- Communicate with Animals
- Communicate with Elemental or Nature Spirit
- Communicate with Objects (psychometry)
- Communicate with Plants
- Control Animals
- Control Elemental or Nature Spirit
- Create or Ignore Difficult Terrain
- Create or Ignore Elements
- Fly
- Gain Animal Senses or Heighten Existing Senses
- Grow Plants
- Heal Living
- Heal Self
- Hibernate
- Levitate
- Locate Animals, Plants, or Minerals
- Meld into Element (Air, Earth, Fire, Water)

- Omen Reading (by studying natural phenomena)
- Pass without Trace
- Release Souls/Spirits (frees bound souls or spirits)
- Remove Disease
- Slay Undead (may only damage powerful undead)
- Slow Aging (target physically ages at a reduced rate)
- Summon Animal
- Summon Elemental or Nature Spirit
- Summon Food or Water
- Summon Natural Barrier (thorn bushes, rocks, etc.)
- Summon Positive Energy Spirit (angel, etc.)
- Summon Weather
- Swim Faster
- Walk on Water

NECROMANCY (NEGATIVE ENERGY MAGIC)

- Banish Positive Energy
- Cause Disease
- Curse
- Communicate with Ghosts or Spirits of the Dead
- Control Ghosts or Spirits of the Dead
- Control Undead
- Create Undead
- Drain and Store Health
- Drain and Store Psychic Energy
- Drain and Store Souls
- Drain and Store Youth
- Immortality (can only die by violence, not old age)
- Locate Ghosts or Spirits of the Dead
- Locate Undead
- Omen Reading (by studying blood, guts, and organs)
- Raise Dead (must be recent)
- Reincarnation (soul is placed into a different body)

- Resurrection (no time limit on how long dead)
- Slay Living
- Slay Ghosts or Spirits
- Speed Aging (target ages at an accelerated rate)
- Summon Ghosts or Spirits
- Summon Negative Energy Spirits (demons, etc.)
- Summon Undead
- Wither Limb (rendering it crippled and/or useless)

TRANSMUTATION (SHAPECHANGING MAGIC)

- Modify Self (partial change, minor)
- Modify Objects (partial change, minor)
- Modify Others (partial change, minor)
- Transform Self (total change, major)
- Transform Objects (total change, major)
- Transform Others (total change, major)

APPENDIX 3: PSYCHIC TALENTS

Psychic talents are innate mental talents that are with a human or monster from birth. However, awareness (much less mastery) may not come until much later, such as with the onset of puberty, as the result of a traumatic brain injury, accidentally unlocked through hypnosis, by experimenting with the occult, etc.

Only gods will have access to all psychic talents. Major supernatural beings will have many, while lesser supernatural beings and humans usually only a few. The number of talents an individual has has nothing to do with how powerful those talents are. Someone with only one talent could be the world's greatest psychic medium, for example, while someone with five or six talents could be terrible at all of them.

Not all psychic talents are created equal and some may only have situational value, rather than be something used on a daily basis. Using talents tends to quickly drain humans depending on how experienced they are with using them. Also, remember that it is more costly for energy beings to project their talents into the physical world than it is to use them in the astral or ethereal planes (or other non-physical dimensions), and the same is true of humans trying to project theirs beyond our physical reality.

Here is a list of common psychic talents:

- Alter Emotion (one step at a time)
- Alter Perceptions/Senses of Others (Create hallucinations)
- Astral Projection
- Bilocation (Ability to be in two places at the same time)
- Cause Seizure/Death in Others (Ability to paralyze or kill with the mind, think *Scanners*)
- Channel Ghost or Spirit (Psychic Mediumship)
- Clairaudience (Hear what others say at a distance)
- Clairvoyance (See what others do at a distance)
- Create or Remove Mental Illness
- Control Others (Mind Control)
- Enhanced Senses (Cannot be surprised, etc.)
- ESP (Extra-Sensory Perception)
- Heal Self or Others (Psychic Surgery)
- Influence Others (Implant Hypnotic Suggestions)
- Locate Energy Beings (and Hide from Same)
- Lucid Dreaming (Control dreams)
- Mind Reading (Hear other's thoughts)
- Modify Memory (Permanently or temporarily)
- Postcognition (Ability to see events *after* they have happened)
- Precognition (Ability to see events *before* they happen)
- Psychic Surgery (healing by the power of thought)
- Psychokinesis (aka telekinesis, the ability to move objects with the mind)
- Psychometry (Read objects to gain insights on past owners)
- Pyrokinesis (Ability start fires with the mind)
- Quicken Self (Increase movement for short bursts)
- Read Auras (See the health/power of an individual or object presented as colors surrounding them)
- See the Invisible (See things made invisible by magic or psychic powers, like energy beings)
- Telepathy (One-way or two-way)

APPENDIX 4: SUPERNATURAL POWERS

Supernatural monsters tend to have a specific set of strength and weaknesses which vary by monster type. For example, all energy beings can pass through physical barriers but may be blocked by salt or running water, as well as have their physical manifestations disrupted by iron.

For your convenience when creating new monsters, here is a list of known supernatural strengths and weaknesses:

SUPERNATURAL STRENGTHS

- Breath Weapon (such as dragon fire)
- Can Create New Monsters of Any Type (either as slaves under its control or free-willed)
- Can Create New Monsters of Its Same Type (either as slaves under its control or free-willed)
- Create Avatar* (physical embodiment of one or more aspects of its power)
- Create Ectoplasm
- Curse Others (with its curse and/or a variety of ailments or

bad luck)

- Enhanced Physical Perfection (erasing any scars, tattoos, brands, blemishes)
- Enhanced Senses (such as seeing in pitch darkness, hear conversations across a crowded room, etc.)
- Extra Limbs
- Flight (limited or unlimited, winged or wingless)
- Hypnotic Gaze (implanting suggestions)
- Ignore Physical Barriers (pass through walls, etc.)
- Immortality (can only be killed by misadventure, not old age or disease)
- Immunity to Holy Objects (either all or specific)
- Immunity to Magic (either all or specific)
- Immunity to Physical Damage (either all or specific)
- Immunity to Psychic Abilities (either all or specific)
- Invisible to Humans (not necessarily to animals)
- Jump or Fall Great Distances (minimal to no injury)
- Levitation
- Natural Defenses (claws, fangs, poison, etc.)
- Petrifying Gaze (paralyze or turn others to stone)
- Possess Others
- Resistance to Magic (either all or specific kinds)
- Resistance to Physical Damage (either all or specific kinds)
- Resistance to Psychic Talents (either all or specific kinds)
- Shapechange into Animal, Bird, Fish, and/or Insect
- Shapechange into Human
- Shapechange into Anything* (real or imagined)
- Split Consciousness* (can be in multiple minds)
- Spread Curse and/or Disease
- Super-healing
- Super-strength
- Super-reflexes
- Super-speed
- Telepathy (One-way or two-way)
- Teleportation

- Wall Climbing (like Spider-Man)
- Weather Control

SUPERNATURAL WEAKNESSES

- Believes Itself and/or Its Kind Superior
- Bound to a Specific Area
- Cannot Consume Normal Food/Drink (becomes ill)
- Cannot Cross Running Water (except by bridge, boat, etc.)
- Cannot Enter a Private Residence without Being Invited by a Living Owner or Guest
- Cannot Enter Holy Ground
- Cannot Speak Holy Names
- Casts No Reflection/Cannot Be Photographed
- Casts No Shadow
- Comatose During the Day
- Hurt or Killed by Decapitation
- Hurt or Killed by Dismemberment
- Hurt or Killed by Fire
- Hurt or Killed by Holy Objects
- Hurt or Killed by Iron
- Hurt or Killed by Salt
- Hurt or Killed by Silver
- Hurt or Killed by Sunlight
- Hurt or Killed by Wooden Arrow/Stake
- Must Feed on Blood (can be Animal or Stored Blood)
- Must Feed on Blood (must be Fresh Blood from a Living Human)
- Must Feed on Flesh (can be Animal or other non-human)
- Must Feed on Flesh (must be Human)
- Must Feed on Psychic Energy (either subtly, or as seen in the movie, *Lifeforce*)
- Must Feed on Youth (either subtly, or as seen in the movie, *Captain Kronos, Vampire Hunter*)

- Must Keep Its Oath or Promise (only under specific conditions)
- Must Rest in Its Native Soil to Recharge Its Powers
- Repelled by Garlic
- Repelled by Holy Objects
- Repelled by Love and/or Positive Emotions
- Repelled by Mirrors
- Repelled by Salt
- Repelled by Water
- Unnaturally Ugly (as seen in *Nosferatu*)

Remember, anything a monster is drawn to can be used against it —even if that thing normally makes it stronger, like blood or negative energy. Clever (or desperate) heroes could use the monster's favorite food as bait or poison. Creative exploitation of your monster's strengths and weaknesses always make for a more interesting story.

SPECIAL FREE BOOK OFFER

BOLDLY GO WHERE NO BOOK HAS GONE BEFORE

— FREE EXCLUSIVE SAMPLER —

"BOLD VISIONS of DARK PLACES"

featuring the best new sci-fi, urban fantasy, and more

by USA TODAY bestselling author

JACKSON DEAN CHASE

Get your free book now at

www.JacksonDeanChase.com

ABOUT JACKSON DEAN CHASE

JACKSON DEAN CHASE is a USA TODAY bestselling author and award-winning poet. His fiction has been praised as "irresistible" in *Buzzfeed* and "diligently crafted" in *The Huffington Post*. Jackson's books on writing fiction have helped thousands of authors.

FROM THE AUTHOR: "I've always loved science fiction, fantasy, and horror, but it wasn't until I combined them with pulp thrillers and *noir* that I found my voice as an author. I want to leave my readers breathless, want them to feel the same desperate longing, the same hope and fear my heroes experience as they struggle not just to survive, but to become something more." — JDC

www.JacksonDeanChase.com
jackson@jacksondeanchase.com

amazon.com/author/jacksondeanchase
bookbub.com/authors/jackson-dean-chase
facebook.com/jacksondeanchaseauthor
instagram.com/jacksondeanchase
twitter.com/Jackson_D_Chase

Made in the USA
Middletown, DE
11 December 2019